Intimacy

Henri J. M. Nouwen

HarperSanFrancisco

A Division of HarperCollins*Publishers*

HarperCollins books may be purchased for educational, business, or sales promotional use. For information please write: Special Markets Department, HarperCollins Publishers, 10 East 53rd Street, New York, NY 10022.

HarperCollins Web Site: http://www.harpercollins.com

HarperCollins ®, 📖 ®, and HarperSanFrancisco ™ are trademarks of HarperCollins Publishers Inc.

Library of Congress Cataloging in Publication Data

Nouwen, Henri J M
    Intimacy: essays in pastoral psychology.

    Originally published by Fides Publishers, Notre Dame, Ind.
    Includes bibliographical references.
    1. Pastoral psychology—Addresses, essays, lectures. 2. Pastoral theology—Catholic Church—Addresses, essays, lectures. I. Title
BV4012.N63   1981   253.5   79-79241
ISBN 0-06-066323-5

98 99 00 01 02 RRD H 26 25 24 23 22

To John Eudes

ACKNOWLEDGMENTS

This book is born out of a two-year "visit" to the University of Notre Dame. The many friendships with students and teachers made it very easy for me to overcome the feeling of being a guest and to fully participate in the intense life of this fast-developing campus, which not only reflects but also stimulates the many turbulent changes in feelings, thoughts and actions of modern society.

Without the stimulation and support of many students the following chapters never would have been written. Special thanks are due to Frank Allman, Ray Novaco, Dwight Norwood, Bob Bradley, Joe Ahearn, Mike McCarty, Greg Milmoe and Joseph Wissink, who by their honest reactions, criticisms and corrections helped me to think and rethink, to write and rewrite.

In the preparation of the chapters about the ministry I found great help in the lively discussions with the Holy Cross priests of the University of Notre Dame. In particular I am grateful to Louis Putz, Joe Hoffmann, Joe Simons, David Burrell, John Gerber, Ralph Dunn, Jim Burtchaell, John Dunne, Claude Pomerleau and Don McNeill. By their great sympathy they made me part of their life and community and in many ways tuned me in to the different problems of the priest on campus.

I also would like to express my great thankfulness to the many faculty members and their wives who encouraged me to write and took away the hesitancies of the foreigner in me. John and Mary Alice Santos, Don and Christine Costello, John and Martha Borkowski, and Charles and Carol Allen, offered through their friendship many insights which are expressed in the following pages.

I owe much to Joe Collins for his careful revisions of the manuscript.

Finally, I am grateful to Linda Papas and Mrs. M. J. van der Meer for their secretarial work.

This book is dedicated to John Eudes Bamberger, monk and psychiatrist, eminent guide through the complexities of the inner life.

CONTENTS

INTRODUCTION

The sources of the following chapters are many: teaching, counseling, discussing, chatting, partying, celebrating, and most of all just being around. Each chapter is written because someone—a student, a teacher, a minister, a priest, a religious brother or sister—asked a question. I wrote on different occasions, for different people, with different questions in mind. I wrote not to solve a problem or to formulate a theory but to respond to men and women who wanted to share their struggles in trying to find their vocation in this chaotic world.

Looking back on the variety of questions and concerns that confronted me, I saw a unity in the many subjects that justifies bringing them together in one book. First of all, there is a unity of perspective, which is pastoral. Although the language and the approach might be considered psychological, the perspective is that of a priest who wonders how to understand what he sees in the light of God's work with people. Secondly, there is a unifying theme. It has become increasingly clear to me that underlying the many concerns there was one main question: "How can I find a creative and fulfilling intimacy in my relationship with God and my fellow human beings?" How can one person develop a fruitful intimacy with another person? What does intimacy mean in the life of a celibate priest or in a community of religious? How can we be intimate with God during moments of celebration or silent prayer?

It is not surprising that many of these questions are

1

raised in a university milieu, dominated by young adults. Erik Erikson has stressed how the careful balance between intimacy and distance is the most crucial psychological task of those coming out of their adolescence and trying to develop lasting and productive relationships. Today, however, the struggle for intimacy is no longer limited to one age group. In the midst of a competitive and demanding world, people of all ages have become painfully aware of their deep-seated desire for a place of intimacy. This desire is felt as much by married people and by priests and religious committed to a celibate life as it is by dating students.

Therefore this book can be considered a book about the inner life. It does not deal with the burning issues that have become such a real part of our daily life: inflation, unemployment, crime, hunger, poverty and the threat of nuclear war. But it tries to address itself directly to what seems to pervade all these problems to some degree: people's seldom articulated and often unrecognized desire for a real home in this world. For that reason, I would like to call this a book about intimacy.

The Context

1

From Magic to Faith

RELIGIOUS GROWTH IN PSYCHOLOGICAL PERSPECTIVE

During the year we are exposed to many events, trivial and significant, which usually don't raise questions unless we pay some special attention to them:

A paratrooper, Captain Ridgway, rowed from Cape Cod to Ireland with his friend. Overwhelmed by the greatness of the ocean and the incredible forces of nature, he found that the medal given to him by the Cape Codders kept him together and gave him words to pray.

One priest, smiling, said to another priest as they left a packed college church at the end of the semester, "The finals are the best proof that man is basically religious."

Little Johnny says, "Hey, Dad, you can't make President Kennedy alive. But God can, can't He? Cause he can do everything!" And we think: "Isn't little Johnny cute?"

You read about an astronaut, symbol of modern science, smuggling a cross into orbit, and you just don't know what to think about it.

Or you meet a student, coming from a deeply religious family where God was the source of strength and happiness, suddenly asking questions so deep and fundamental that everything that had happened before seems completely irrelevant to him.

Then you read about a group of young men leaving their good jobs, their comfortable homes and sometimes even their families to go to the most desperate places of this world, to live with people they don't even as yet know.

What about all this? Magic or Faith? Superstition or contact with ultimate reality? Something to avoid or to aspire to? To clarify these questions let us look at the life of a man from the time he is folded in the safe womb of his mother to the moment he is walking around, broad-shouldered, with his thumbs pushed behind his leather belt, curiously looking around at this world and what lies beyond. We will call this trip "from Magic to Faith." We all make this trip, and it might be worthwhile to look at it from a distance.

In each phase of a man's life we will stress one particular aspect of our development which is a constituent of a mature religious sentiment.

A. *The first five years of life*

During the first five years of life we have to take three big steps out of the magical world in which we are born.

I. During the first 18 months we come to the somewhat frustrating discovery that we are not the center of the world.

Most of you will agree that there are people and things outside of us which will continue to exist even when we don't. This is, however, not so self-evident as it seems. It is only through a long and often frustrating experience that we are able to discover the objective world. As a baby in the mother's womb, everything is there for us; mother is a part of ourself. Later, it can be quite a painful experience to discover that our cry does not create the milk, that our smile does not produce the mother, that our needs do not evoke their own satisfaction. Only gradually do we discover our mother as the other, as not just a part of ourself. Every time we experience that we are not ruling the world by our feelings, thoughts and actions, we are forced to realize that there are other persons, things and events which have their autonomy.

Therefore, the first step out of the magical world is the discovery of an objective reality. It can happen that we reach this objectivity only partially. Although we slowly unfold and become able to stand on our own feet and point to the things around us as objective realities available for our curious mind, this may not happen so easily in the religious dimension. Many mature, successful men in this life often might still treat God as part of themselves. God is the factotum which comes in handy in times of illness, shock, final exams, in every situation in which we feel insecure. And if it does not work, the only reaction may be to cry louder. Far from becoming the Other, whose existence does not depend on mine, he might remain the easy frame which fits best around the edges of my security. Great anxiety, caused by internal or external storms, can sometimes force us to regress to this level of religion. This regression may even save our life, as it did Captain Ridgway's. It gives us something to hold on to, a medal or a candle which can keep us together. It may be a very helpful form of religion; but certainly it is not a mature form of religion.

II. The second step out of our magical world is the formation of the language. Somewhere between our 18th month of life and our 3rd birthday we started mumbling our first sounds which slowly developed into words, sentences, and a language. Although it may be disappointing that there are things around us which do not belong to us, by words we can take revenge, because our first words give us a mysterious power over things. Like an American who is excited to discover that his first French word, *garçon*, really brings the waiter to his table, the child experiences not so much the mastery of words but mastery of objects. It takes quite a while before we can detach the word from the object and give it a symbolic function.

The magical word gives us power not only over objects but also over our own instinctual impulses. Before we had words we couldn't resist the temptation of grabbing flowers in daddy's garden. But by the word "flower" we became able to substitute the act of grabbing and touching, and with our hands clasped together at our back we could then say: "nice flower, no touch." [1]

Well, religion is full of words. Long litanies, exclamations and often-repeated formulas play a very important role in many religions. What concerns us here is that this use of words often does not transcend the magical phase. Instead of being the free and creative expression of deep realities communicable to our fellow man, the words may become a substitute for reality, a subtle form of power over the capricious movements of our gods, our devils, or our own impulses.

Is there not something of this magical world left in us if we feel that we will be saved if we say our prayers every day, or if we at least keep the custom of the three Hail Marys before going to bed? It seems difficult to overcome this word-magic. We feel pretty good if we have fulfilled our obliga-

---

[1] Selma H. Fraiberg, *The Magic Years* (Charles Scribner's Sons: 1959).

tion, mumbled our table prayers, raced through our rosary or recited our breviary. We seem to be saying, "God cannot do anything to us now. We did what he asked us to do, and now it is his turn to pay us back." Our prayers give us some power over God, instead of engaging us in a real dialogue.

III. The third step out of the magical world is the formation of our conscience. This is the great event between our third and fifth years. When we had learned that objects existed outside ourselves which kept existing even if we did not, and when we had experienced that words were not omnipotent tools to manipulate the world around us, we were still confronted with a much more important step: the step from daddy to us. "I am not going to hit my nasty little sister, not because Daddy does not like that, but because I don't like it, because it is bad." The external disciplinary agent, daddy, mommy, priest etc., slowly is converted into an internal policeman.

Conscience becomes possible by the process of identification. We develop the capacity to interiorize certain aspects of the personality of another person, to make them a part of ourselves. In the case of moral development, we take over judgments, standards and values of beloved persons and incorporate them into our own personality.

Or is there something else happening at the same time? During those first four years of life we felt that daddy could do everything, that he was omnipotent, that he could solve all the problems and lift all the weights. In our fantasy daddy is the greatest athlete in the world, he builds houses, writes books, creates bicycles and is able to get everything for me, if only he wants to. Well, we became disappointed sooner or later. Daddy turns out to be a square, after all. We couldn't really depend on him any longer. How could we solve this problem?

Interiorization might not solve the whole problem. The need for an omnipotent Father who gives us love, shelter and protection, in whose arms we can hide and feel safe, might simply be too intense. The magical father couldn't be done without, we needed him too much, and therefore, he stayed with us in another name: GOD. And so we thought that if daddy could not make President Kennedy live again, at least God could do it.

When Sigmund Freud wrote his *Future of an Illusion*, he irritated and deeply disturbed the faithful, by saying that religion is the continuation of intantile life and that God is the projection of the ever-present desire for shelter.

Freud's task was to cure people, that is, to make them become more mature. And looking at the many people in his office in Vienna who suffered from their religion more than they were saved by it, he tried to unmask their projections. The psychiatrist Rumke summarizes Freud's position when he writes: "When man matures completely he realizes that his God image, often a father-God image, is a reincarnation of the infantile worldly father, loved and feared. God is apparently no more than a projection. If that which blocks his growth is taken away, the image fades. Man distinguishes good from evil according to his own standards. He has conquered the remainder of his neurosis, which was all that his religion was." [2] What is important in this context is that Freud was not altogether wrong. We often stay in this magical and infantile world in which God is as nice to have around as the comforting blanket of Linus in "Peanuts." For

---

[2] H. C. Rümke, *The Psychology of Unbelief* (Sheed & Ward: 1962).

many, religion is really not very much more than Freud found it to be, and for all of us, so many of our religious experiences are clothed in images of childhood that it is often very difficult to say where our infantilism ends and our religion begins.

It seems appropriate here to ask a critical question: Is the idea of God an infantile prolongation of our ideal father image, or is our receptivity to the child-father idea the result of our more profound and primary relationship with God? Indeed the basic criticism of Freud proposed by the German psychiatrist Binswanger is a reversal: God is not the prolongation of the child's relationship with his dad, but the child's feeling for his dad is a concretizing of an idea born of his most fundamental relation to his Creator. In other words, we couldn't love our father if God had not loved us first. But here we have left the field of psychology.[3]

In one way we have to agree with Freud: in so far as our God is a pure surrogate for our conscience and a preventative to the development of a rational mind, a mature self and an autonomous individual, it is only a sign of good health and insight to throw our God out as a disease called neurosis. It is even sad to notice how few have the courage to do this.

Healthy development means a gradual movement out of the magical world. Even when the development takes place in other areas, our religion easily remains on this immature level. In that case, God remains the magical pacifier whose existence depends on ours. Prayers remain tools to manipulate him in our direction and religion is nothing more than a big, soft bed on which we doze away and deny the hardships of life. Our religious sentiment will never be mature

---

[3] H. C. Rümke, *ibid.*

1) if God is not the Other, 2) if prayer is not a dialogue, and 3) if religion is not a source of creative autonomy.

B. *School age: 5-12 years*

When we were about five years old we went to school. In the small unit of our family the most essential behavioral patterns were pretty well established. Our first experiences of trust, happiness, fear, friendship, joy and disappointment and our first reactions to these experiences took place in our parental home. But then we entered a new world. In school we met other boys and girls who also had parents and homes, and then we had to find out if what we learned at home really worked. In many ways our years in grade school were years in which our major patterns of behavior were fortified, modified, enlarged or disrupted, years in which we experienced success and failure in a larger society than we were used to during the first years of our lives.

Religion in our society is generally a private affair. As soon as we heard about the new math, the history of man, as soon as we learned how to do things ourselves and how to be master of our world, the chance was great that religion became isolated as a separate reality, good for Sunday and the pious hour of the week but not really related to all the new things we heard about this and other worlds. Allport says maturity comes only when a growing intelligence somehow is animated by the desire not to suffer arrested development, but to keep pace with the intake of relevant experience. "In many people, so far as the religious sentiment is concerned, this inner demand is absent. Finding their childhood religion to have comforting value and lacking outside pressure, they cling to an essentially juvenile formulation."[4]

---

[4] Gordon Allport, *The Individual and his Religion* (Macmillan: 1950).

A mature religion is integral in nature—that means that it is flexible enough to integrate all new knowledge within its frame of reference and keep pace with all the new discoveries of the human mind. It indeed takes the cross into the space craft. Going to school means starting on the road to science, and if religion does not follow the same road with an open and critical eye, the grown man who flies the ocean in superjets might be religiously still content with his tricycle. Essential for mature religion is the constant willingness to shift gears, to integrate new insights and to revise our positions.

C. Adolescence: 12-18 years

With adolescence, we entered into a new and very critical phase of our development. Some of us might have experienced a sudden and dramatic change, others gradually entered the new realities hardly noticing the entry.

Suddenly or gradually, we were confronted with the fact that not only is life outside of us very complicated but life inside of us is just as complicated, or even more so. Until this time we were very curious about all the things going on around us, were excited by all the new things we saw and heard; but then we sensed deep and, often, very strange and disturbing feelings inside. New, often dark, urges seemed to push us without our understanding. We were overwhelmed by feelings of intense joy and happiness, so much so that we didn't know what it meant. Or we were victims of a wish to die, to kill, to hurt, to destroy. We felt that we were torn apart sometimes by the most conflicting feelings and ideas; love and hate, desire to embrace and desire to kill; desire to give and desire to take.

Perhaps we touch here one of the most important crossroads of our religious development. The question is: can we accept and understand our inner conflicts in such a way that by clarification and understanding they become a source of maturation of our religious sentiment? Very often we fail. Very often religion has become identified with cleanliness, purity, the perfect life—and every feeling which seems to throw black spots on our white sheet seems to be antireligious. In that case we cannot allow ourselves to have strong sexual urges and cruel fantasies and aggressive desires. Religion says: "No!" Do not curse, do not steal, do not kill, do not masturbate, do not gossip, do not, do not, do not . . . Then teachers who tell us to be nice, obedient and lovable start to irritate us no end. Nobody really seems to understand this strange new world of internal feelings which make us feel solemnly unique but, at the same time, horribly lonesome.

Many of us remember how deeply we wanted understanding, how difficult it was to express ourselves and how few people really were close to us. A feeling of shame and guilt often made us feel terribly lonesome and we felt that we were hypocrites whom nobody would love if they really knew how we felt. Many things are possible in this period. We might feel that religion was so oppressive and depressive, so far away from all our experience, so authoritarian and negativistic that the only way of resolving the conflict was to break away from it. Some became sick of the shouting priest in the pulpit, others never felt any understanding for their disturbing feelings or could no longer stand the obvious hypocrisy of many churchgoers, and many dropped away—some slowly, others in open rebellion.

But there is another reaction, perhaps more harmful. This is the tendency to deny and repress drastically the other side, the dark wishes, the unwelcome shadow. Then we are saying, "After all, we are clean, pure, sinless, and we want to keep our record spotless." We want to stay in complete control of ourselves, never have an evil thought, never curse, never get drunk, never fail, but always remain perfect, saintly and, in a way, so self-content that we don't leave anything to God to be saved. We walk through life as if we had swallowed an Easter candle, rigid and tense, always afraid that things will get out of hand.

This reaction is just as harmful as open rebellion, or even more so, because it blocks our way to religious maturation. But there is a way to maturity in which we can say, "Sure, I have weak spots but that does not make me weak. I have ugly thoughts but that does not make me ugly." This is the realization that we have to tolerate the weeds in order to have good wheat. If we try to eradicate all the weeds we might also pull out the precious wheat. A man who is never mad nor angry can never be passionately in favor of anything either. A man who never loses his temper might have nothing worthwhile to lose after all; he who is never down seldom enjoys himself either. He who never takes a risk might never fail, but he also will never succeed.

It is very difficult for each of us to believe in Christ's words, "I did not come to call the virtuous, but sinners. . . ." Perhaps no psychologist has stressed the need of self-acceptance as the way to self-realization so much as Carl Jung. For Jung, self-realization meant the integration of the shadow. It is the growing ability to allow the dark side of our personality to enter into our awareness and thus prevent a one-sided life in which only that which is presentable to the outside world is considered as a real part of ourselves. To come to an inner unity, totality and wholeness, every part of our self should be accepted and integrated. Christ represents the light in us. But Christ was crucified between two murderers and we cannot deny them, and certainly not the murderers who live in us.

This is a task for life, but during our adolescence we had a real chance to test our religious sentiment in this respect. The conflict is obvious; the solution is not rebellion nor repression, but integration.

D. The young adult

Meanwhile, we went to college. What happens in college? College is the period between homes. We have left our parental home and have not yet committed ourselves to a home of our own. We have gone a safe distance from all things Mom and Dad always had to say but we also keep a safe distance from those who want to take away this wonderful vacation from home life. We don't have to worry any more about how to find a compromise between our own ideas and feelings and those of our parents, but on the other hand, we are not yet responsible to any one person in particular. We feel that the time of being educated is over but we are not quite ready to start educating others. In short, we live between two homes, and in a certain way this is the period of the greatest freedom of our life.

In college we also develop a new way of thinking. We learn a scientific approach; the key term is: hypothesis; the criterion: probability; and the tool: experimentation. Only on the basis of an experiment are we willing to accept and reject, and only with a sense of relativity do we want to speak about certainty. For our religious development the college years can become the most ideal time to make our religious ideas and values from "second-hand fittings into first-hand fittings" (Allport). We may develop enough self-acceptance and creative distance to do some responsible experimentation.

During the college years, a new important aspect of a mature religious sentiment can develop: "I can be sure without being cocksure" (Allport). As we enter college we take with us many religious concepts and ideas which seemed obvious, and which we never questioned. The question is, whether or not we have the courage to put question marks behind many things; if we can allow ourselves to doubt without losing all grounds. Only he who feels safe in this world can take risks, only he who has a basic trust in the value of life is free to ask many questions without feeling threatened. Trust creates the possibility of a religion of search, which makes a commitment possible without certainty. By the basic trust in the meaning of life we are able to live with a hypothesis, without the need of absolute certainty.

The man who never had any religious doubts during his college years probably walked around blindfolded; he who never experimented with his traditional values and ideas was probably more afraid than free; he who never put to a test any of dad's and mom's advice probably never developed a critical mind; and he who never became irritated by the many ambiguities, ambivalences and hypocrisies in his religious milieu probably never was really satisfied with anything either. But he who did, took a risk. The risk of embarrassing not only his parents but also his friends, the risk of feeling alienated from his past and of becoming irritated by everything religious, even the word "God." The risk even of the searing loneliness which Jesus Christ suffered when He cried, "God, my God, why have you forsaken me?"

In college we can often discover, with pain and frustration, that a mature religious man is very close to the agnostic, and often we have difficulty in deciding which name expresses better our state of mind: agnostic or searching believer. Perhaps they are closer than we tend to think.

E. The adult man

One facet of adulthood which has special significance for our religious attitude is that the mature adult mind is characterized by a unifying philosophy of life. If we could look at our daily life from above, we might wonder what we are so busy for, so excited about, so concerned with. We might ask with Alfie, "After all, what is it all about?" And if there is no real answer to this question, the most honest reaction might be: boredom. Many people who no longer see the meaning of their lives, their daily, often utterly dull, activities, feel bored. Boredom is the dullness of life felt all the way to your stomach. It is the lukewarm quality of daily life, which manifests itself in the repetition of the "I don't care" phrase. Now if we ask ourselves what boredom really means we might say, "It is the isolation of experience." That is to say, we have an experience in life which in no way seems to be connected with the past or the future. Every day seems to be just another day, indifferent, colorless and bleak, just like every other day. This is the mentality in which we need "kicks"—very short, artificially induced upheavals which, for a while, pull us out of our boredom without really giving any meaning to past or future.

Boredom is the disconnected life, filled with thousands of different words, ideas, thoughts and acts which seem like so many pieces of garbage in stagnant waters. Boredom, which so easily leads to depression, often can become a pervasive feeling, a creeping temptation, difficult to shake off. And certainly, if we have finished school and have a family and a job, this feeling of deep boredom might overwhelm us with the question, "So what?" Now we have everything, and we will be dead, gone and forgotten in a couple of years, perhaps only remembered because of our oddities and idiosyncracies!

It is in this perspective that a mature, religious sentiment fulfills a creative function. Because it has a unifying power, it brings together the many isolated realities of life and casts them into one meaningful whole. The thousand disconnected pieces fall together and show a pattern which we couldn't see before. All the individuals in the card section of the stadium don't seem to make sense to each other, but from a certain distance, and in a certain perspective, they form a very meaningful word. Just so in a unifying perspective, the many facets of life prove to belong together and point in a definite direction. That is what we refer to if we say that a mature religion gives meaning to life, gives direction, reveals a goal and creates a task to be accomplished. It can make us leave job, country and family to dedicate our life to the suffering poor. It can make us bury ourselves in silence, isolation and contemplation in a Trappist monastery.

This new perspective is what we can call faith. It does not create new things but it adds a new dimension to the basic realities of life. It brings our fragmented personality into a meaningful whole, unifies our divided self. It is the source of inspiration for a searching mind, the basis for a creative community and a constant incentive for an on-going renewal of life.

So we come to the end of our trip from Magic to Faith. We started folded up in our mother's womb, one with the world in which we lived. We slowly unfolded out of the magical unity into an autonomous existence, in which we discovered that we were not alone but stood in a constant dialogue with our surroundings; and we ended by bringing together all the varieties of life in a new unity—not that of Magic but that of Faith.

Intimacy and sexuality

2

The Challenge to Love

Although I am not writing from the Iron Mountain, I would like to consider this chapter as a "Report on the Possibility and Desirability of Love." For the question is not, What should I do if I find myself in deep love with another stranger in this world? but rather, Can this love ever be a reality at all? Many are asking themselves if we are doomed to remain strangers to each other. Is there a spark of misunderstanding in every intimate encounter, a painful experience of separateness in every attempt to unite, a fearful resistance in every act of surrender? Is there a fatal component of hate in the center of everything we call love?

We probably have wondered in our many lonesome moments if there is one corner in this competitive, demanding world where it is safe to be relaxed, to expose ourselves to someone else, and to give unconditionally. It might be very small and hidden. But if this corner exists, it calls for a search through the complexities of our human relationships in order to find it.

How do we go about this? Our plan is first to describe carefully and understand the two main forms of existing, the form of power and the form of love, or in other words, the taking form and the forgiving form, and secondly to examine how these forms are related to destruction and to creation. Only then are we ready to ask the crucial question: Is love a utopian dream or a possibility within our reach?

A. THE TAKING FORM

Our attention goes first to the taking form of existence, which is the form of power. Let me start by introducing the man who suffers from a constant fear that everything is too much for him. Everything, I mean. It just seems that he is no longer able to keep the many pieces of his life together in a meaningful unity. He is nervous and trembling, tense and restless, and he has lost his usual ability to concentrate and create. He says, "I can't function any longer. Everybody likes me, my friends think a lot of me—but they don't really know me. If they found out who I really am and how I really feel, they wouldn't want to look at me any longer. I know that I often hate instead of love, that I sometimes want to hurt instead of cure, to kill instead of heal. You know, I am a hypocrite." Few people will say this. Perhaps we sometimes say it to ourselves and find ourselves caught in a prison of fear. "If they really knew us, they would stop loving us." It is the fear of being trapped, of being taken.

Let us have a closer look at this all-pervasive taking form.[1] When you take a teacup by its handle, you can keep it at a distance and look at it from all sides. You can make it an obedient instrument in your hands. You can manipulate it in any direction you want. You have complete control over it, for it is in your hands, your power. Many of our human relationships are of this order. When you are mad at a four year

---

[1] Cf., Ludwig Binswanger, *Grundformen und Erkenntnis Menschlichen Daseins* (Max Niehans Verlag Zürich: 1953), pp. 266-281.

old and take him by his ear and shake his head like a teacup, he feels offended, humiliated, treated like an object. When in a hazing party, you take a freshman by his nose, pull his leg, or pinch his cheeks, he feels taken. But worse than these physical forms is the mental form in which we can take our fellow man. We can take him by his vulnerable spot, his hidden weakness, and make him an object at which we can look from a distance, which we can turn around and lead to the place we want it to go. You see how this form of taking is a form of power. It has the structure of blackmailing, in which we keep the other's weakness behind our back, until the moment we can use it against him at the time he blocks our way.

There are too many illustrations in our life to deny the dominating role of this taking form of existence. When you sit together and talk in a free and relaxed fashion about a friend you like very much, it might happen that a stranger walks in and says: "Who are you talking about? About Mary? Oh, that sexpot . . ." You freeze. Mary has become an object, a thing, a piece of conversation, and the dialogue dies and often is perverted into a verbal combat. When a psychologist revels in discovering that his patient is a classic example of an obsessive neurotic and sends him home with the new label, gratified by his good diagnosis, he takes him by his weakness and substitutes classification for cure. When people go through your life history to check your past and find your weak spot which can be used against you, should you move in a direction opposite of their power, they operate in the taking form. The Russian author, Daniel, one of the victims of a recent writers' trial, describes in vivid terms how the revelation of a dark spot in someone's past can drive him into isolation, despair and finally total disintegration. Knowing someone's past can be the most lethal weapon in human relationships, which can bring about shame, guilt, moral and even physical death.

But we don't need such dramatic examples. Is not every student, who fills out application forms for graduate schools, and every professor, who writes letters of recommendation, obedient to the taking structure of our life? We are judged, evaluated, tested, and graded, diagnosed and classified from the time our parents compared our first walk with a little neighbor's. Gradually, as time goes on, we realize that our permanent record is building its own life, independent of ours. It is really not so amazing that we often feel caught, taken, and used for purposes not our own. The main concern then becomes not who I am but who I am considered to be, not what I think, but what others think of me.

In this taking existence we find ourselves operating in terms of power, motivated by fear. We are armed to our teeth, carefully following the movements of the other, waiting to hit back at the right moment and in the vulnerable spot. If we don't, we just might miss the right job, the good grad school, the assignment in Alaska (which we had hoped for during the Vietnam crisis), or even the man or woman we hoped to marry. And so, often in very subtle forms we envelop ourselves in the cocoon of our taking world.

Even understanding people, which seems the opposite of taking them, becomes stained by power. "Psychological understanding" then means having an idea about the hidden motives of people. It is like saying: "You don't have to tell me. I know that fellow." Hours of therapy and counseling can be wasted by the client trying to figure out what technique the counselor uses. Isn't this true also for many dating relationships? Sometimes it seems that a boy feels more relaxed in the classroom than when he is alone with a girl. Instead of feeling free to give his affection, express freely his moods and concerns to the girl he loves, he is more self-conscious than ever, wants to make the right remark at the right time, and is everything but spontaneous. What looks from a distance like love is often, at a closer look, fear. I am saying, "I don't want to become a pawn, to be pushed around. I want to keep control over the situation. And after all—it is always better to drop than to be dropped."

All this leaves us with the suspicion that the reality which we call "love" is nothing other than a blanket to cover the real fact that a man and a woman conquer each other in a long, subtle skirmish of taking movements in which one is always the winner who manipulates the other in the patterns of his or her life. Love seems to be unmasked as another taking of our fellow man and exercising of our subtle but pervasive power over him.

If this is true, destruction becomes an inescapable aspect of our existence, for the taking form of life means that our weakness can always be held against us and that there is no place in life where we are safe. Thomas Merton in his study about nonviolence has shown how this taking mode of existence is based on the concept of the irreversibility of evil. Your mistakes, failures, and offenses are unchangeable elements on the record of your life. Evil then is definitive and unchangeable. The only solution for the irreversible is its destruction. If evil cannot be reversed and forgiven, the only thing those living the taking mode can do with it is to cut it out, to uproot it, to burn it to ashes. In its full consequences this means that tenderness, sympathy, and love can only be considered as weaknesses to be eliminated, and that every mistake is final and unforgiveable. Then a misplaced gesture becomes a haunting memory, a bitter word creates an excruciating remorse, and a faithless moment leads to despair and destruction of life.

These are the dynamics of war and hate. If we look at the thousands of people suffering in mental institutions, the millions of children crushed in the conflict between their parents, the endless number of people separated from each other and left alone, we wonder if anybody can ever escape the taking form of our existence. It is the form of power which brings destruction unless the power is ours.

In this perspective, imprisoned in the vicious circle of taking, power and final destruction, we find ourselves doomed to the impossibility of love. Not without sarcasm in his voice, the man of power will say: "Love, peace and forgiveness are the dreams of those who have not yet entered the vicious circle. But wait until the day when their most primitive impulse to survive will speak its irresistible language. Then they will not only take life, they will grab it."

B. THE FORGIVING FORM, WHICH IS THE FORM OF LOVE

But the man who dared to trust us said: "If my friends found out who I really am and how I really feel, they would not look at me any longer, they would spit on me and leave me alone with my hypocrisy." This man has drastically broken through the closed circle. Somehow he has jumped far beyond the reasonable and has broken through the walls of shame. He has believed that confession is a possibility. When a man cries, when the walls of his self-composure break down and he is able to express his deepest despair, weakness, hate and jealousy, his meanness and inner division, he somewhere believes that we will not take and destroy him. As if a voice told him: "Don't be afraid to tell."

Maybe we remember the few occasions in our life in which we were able to show someone we love our real self: not only our great successes but also our weaknesses and pains, not only our good intentions but also our bitter motives, not only our radiant face but also our dark shadow. It takes a lot of courage, but it might just open a new horizon, a new way of living. It is this breaking through the closed circle, often described as a conversion experience, which may come suddenly and unexpectedly or slowly and gradually. People might call us a crazy idealist, an unrealistic dreamer, a first class romanticist, but it does not touch us very deeply because we know with a new form of certainty which we had never experienced before that peace, forgiveness, justice, and inner freedom are more than mere words. Conversion is the discovery of the possibility of love.

How can we understand this loving form of existence in which the taking form is transcended? Love is not based on the willingness to listen, to understand problems of others, or to tolerate their otherness. Love is based on the mutuality of the confession of our total self to each other. This makes us free to declare not only: "My strength is your strength" but also: "Your pain is my pain, your weakness is my weakness, your sin is my sin." It is in this intimate fellowship of the weak that love is born. When the exposure of one's deepest dependency becomes an invitation to share this most existential experience, we enter a new area of life. For in this sharing of weakness violence can be overcome. When we are ready to throw stones—words can be as sharp as stones—someone just may have the courage to cry out: "He who is without sin, let him throw the first stone."

If we are willing to believe that the wheat can only come to full maturity if we allow the weeds to exist in the same field, we don't have to be afraid of every conflict and avoid every argument. It is here where love creates a smile, and where humor can be soft instead of cynical. You know the situation. John and Sally walk in the park. After a ten minute exposition by John about Hegel, Kierkegaard, Camus, Sartre and some other of his recent authors, there is a long silence. Sally asks, "John, do you care for me?" John becomes a little irritated, "Sure I do, but I wanted to know what you think about existentialism." Sally: "John I don't want to marry a philosopher. I want to marry you." John becomes mad. "Don't be so silly and stupid, if we can't have a decent conversation, how can we ever get along?" Sally: "There is little more to love than a decent conversation, and I just don't want to be another of your classmates."

Well, they had a short walk that evening. But perhaps later they could laugh about it and say, "At least we were not afraid to show our real feelings." If John and Sally would have been only sweet, understanding and agreeing with each other they might have doubted if they really were free to love. And it is exactly there, where love becomes visible.

Let us examine some characteristics of love. Love first of all is *truthful*. In the fellowship of the weak the truth creates the unshakable base on which we feel free to move. Truth means primarily the full acceptance of our basic human condition, which says that no man has power over any other man. Faithfulness is only possible if constantly guided by the truth of the human situation which prevents us from fictitiousness, shallowness, and simulation.

The second characteristic of love is its *tenderness*. Perhaps nowhere does it become so clear that love transcends the taking form than in its tenderness. In love hands don't take, grasp or hold. They caress. Caressing is the possibility of human hands to be tender. The careful touch of the hand makes for growth. Like a gardner who carefully touches the flowers to enable the light to shine through and stimulate growth, the hand of the lover allows for the full self-expression of the other. In love the mouth does not bite, devour or destroy. It kisses. A kiss is not to take in, but to allow for the full and fearless surrender. In love the eyes don't trap the stranger's body through a sartrian keyhole, nor do they arouse shame by the feeling of being exposed as Noah felt when his son Ham looked at his naked body; but in love the eyes cover the other's body with the warm radiation of an admiring smile as an expression of tenderness.

Finally and most importantly, love asks for a total *disarmament*. The encounter in love is an encounter without weapons. Perhaps the disarmament in the individual encounter is more difficult than international disarmament. We are very able to hide our guns and knives even in the most intimate relationship. An old bitter memory, a slight suspicion about motives, or a small doubt can be as sharp as a knife held behind our back as a weapon for defense in case of attack. Can we ever meet a fellow man without any protection? Reveal ourselves to him in our total vulnerability? This is the heart of our question. Are man and woman able to exclude the power in their relationship and become totally available for each other? When the soldier sits down to eat he lays down his weapons, because eating means peace and rest. When he stretches out his body to sleep he is more vulnerable than ever. Table and bed are the two places of intimacy where love can manifest itself in weakness. In love men and women take off all the forms of power, embracing each other in total disarmament. The nakedness of their body is only a symbol of total vulnerability and availability.

When the physical encounter of men and women in the intimate act of intercourse is not an expression of their total availability to each other, the creative fellowship of the weak is not yet reached. Every sexual relationship with built-in reservations, with mental restrictions or time limits, is still part of the taking structure. It means "I want you now, but not tomorrow. I want something from you, but I don't want *you*." Love is limitless. Only when men and women give themselves to each other in total surrender, that is, with their whole person for their whole life, can their encounter bear full fruits. When through the careful growth of their relationship men and women have come to the freedom of total disarmament, their giving also becomes for-giving, their nakedness does not evoke shame but desire to share, and their ultimate vulnerability becomes the core of their mutual strength. New life is born in the state of total vulnerability—this is the mystery of love. Power kills. Weakness creates. It creates autonomy, self-awareness and freedom. It creates openness to give and receive in mutuality. And finally it creates the good ground on which new life can come to full development and maturity. This explains why the highest safeguard for the physical, mental and spiritual health of the child is not primarily the attention paid to the child but the unrestricted love of the parents for each other.

If the taking form of existence were the only possibility, destruction would be our fate. But if love can be found, creation can exist. Because love is based, as Merton says, on the belief in the reversibility of evil. Evil then is not final and unchangeable. Ghandi's concept of nonviolence was essentially based on his conviction that forgiveness could change every enemy into a friend, that in hatred love is hidden, in despair hope, in doubt faith, in evil good, in sin redemption. Love is an act of forgiving in which evil is converted to good and destruction into creation. In the truthful, tender, and disarmed encounter of love man is able to create.

In this perspective it becomes clear that the sexual act is a religious act. Out of the total disarmament of man on his cross, exposing himself in his extreme vulnerability, the new man arises and manifests himself in freedom. Is it not exactly in this same act of self-surrender that we find our highest fulfillment which expresses itself in the new life we create? Religion and sexuality, which in the past have been so often described as opponents, merge into one and the same reality when they are seen as an expression of the total self-surrender in love.

C. The Possibility of Love

Having described the taking form and the loving form, the form which can destroy by power and the form which can create through forgiving, we have to return to our original question: "Is love a utopian dream or a possibility within our reach?" Let us start here by saying that our life is often a very painful fluctuation between the two desires to take and to forgive. We want to be ambitious and competitive but sometimes we want to forgive. We want strength and successes, but sometimes we feel a desire to confess our other side. We want to kill, but also to cure, to hurt but also to help. Although the world in which we live keeps suggesting that realism is an outlook on life based on power, confusing but at the same time attractive prophets keep saying that there is another possible alternative, the alternative of love. They all seem to ask for conversion, change of mind. But we don't know if we really can take the risk.

And we have good reasons to be afraid. Love means openness, vulnerability, availability and confession. When our friend says, "If my friends found out how I really feel, if I would show my real self, then they would no longer love me but hate me"—he speaks about a real possibility. It is very risky to be honest, because someone just might not respond with love, but take us by our weak spot and turn it against ourselves. Our confession might destroy us. Revealing our past failures and present ambivalences can make us losers. We can be thrown away in a gesture of contempt. This is not only a possibility but a cruel fact in the lives of many who feel that love and forgiveness is a utopian fantasy of flower children.

It is obvious that the taking structure is so much a part of our existence that we cannot avoid it. Don't ask the telephone operator how she is feeling today. Don't start a conversation about the prayer life of the man from whom you want to buy some stamps at the post office. Don't ask your teacher about his sexual behavior. You destroy human communication because you want to play a game without rules, which means no game at all. We are wise enough to prefer in most situations the taking form. Wise as the oyster who keeps his hard shell tightly closed to protect his tender and vulnerable self. Our problem therefore is not how we can completely annihilate the taking structure of life but whether there is any possibility at all to transcend that structure, to open our shell even when it is only somewhat, somewhere, somehow, sometime.

How often is the intimate encounter of two persons an expression of their total freedom? Many people are driven into each other's arms in fear and trembling. They embrace each other in despair and loneliness. They cling to each other to prevent worse things from happening. Their sleep together is only an expression of their desire to escape the threatening world, to forget their deep frustration, to ease for a minute the unbearable tension of a demanding society, to experience some warmth, protection, and safety. Their privacy does not create a place where they both can grow in freedom and share their mutual discoveries, but a fragile shelter in a storming world.

But can it be anything else, we wonder, if the only real and final solution to life is death. If we don't know where we come from or where we are going, if life is a trembling little flame between two darknesses, if we are thrown into this existence only to be swallowed by it, then being secure seems more pathological than real. In that case there is nothing else left for us to do but to try to survive and use all possible power to keep the flame burning. Is this cowardice? Perhaps. But it often seems better to be a coward than to be dead.

Here the psychologist stops and the philosopher finishes his last sentences with a question mark. Here we also should stop—unless someone is able to cut through the vicious circle. Indeed, it seems that sometimes in the depths of our despair and in the loneliness of our prison, we do not become hardened and bitter but open and sensitive for the voice of a new man. Those who want to hear him can hear him and those who want to read him can read him. To many he is a source of irritation and anger, for a few a sign of hope. In ecstasy the new man proclaims:

> Something which has existed since the beginning, that we have heard and have seen with our own eyes; that we have watched and touched with our hands: . . . this is our subject. . . . God is light, there is no darkness in him at all . . . . If we live our lives in the light, as he is in the light, we are in union with one another . . . (1 John 1:1-7).

Suddenly everything is converted into its opposite. Darkness into light, enslavement into freedom, death into life, taking into giving, destruction into creation and hate into love. With an irresistible strength the voice breaks through the vicious circle of our existence saying:

> Let us love one another since love comes from God . . . (1 John 4:7). In love there can be no fear, but fear is driven out by perfect love: because to fear is to expect punishment, and anyone who is afraid is still imperfect in love (1 John 4:18). (But) God is greater than our heart (1 John 3:20). We have to love, because he loved us first (1 John 4:19).

What else does this mean besides the redeeming revelation that love *is* a possibility? Perhaps the best definition of revelation is the uncovering of the truth that it is safe to love. The walls of our anxiety, our anguish, our narrowness are broken down and a wide endless horizon is shown. "We have to love, because he loved us first." It is safe to embrace in vulnerability because we both find ourselves in loving hands. It is safe to be available because someone told us that we stand on solid ground. It is safe to surrender because we will not fall into a dark pit but enter a welcoming home. It is safe to be weak because we are surrounded by a creative strength.

To say and live this is a new way of knowing. We are not surrounded by darkness but by light. He who knows this light will see it. The cripple will walk, the deaf hear, the mute speak, the blind see, and the mountains move. Someone has appeared to us and said: The sign of love is the sign of weakness: A baby wrapped in swaddling clothes and lying in a manger. That is the glory of God, the peace of the world and the good will of all men.

I could not find any other language than this to express that love has become a possibility. If there is a need for a new morality it is the morality which teaches us the fellowship of the weak as a human possibility. Love then is not a clinging to each other in the fear of an oncoming disaster but an encounter in a freedom that allows for the creation of new life. This love cannot be proved. We can only be invited to it and find it to be true by an engaging response. As long as we experience the Christian life as a life which puts restrictions on our freedom of expression, we have perverted and inverted its essence. The core message of Christianity is exactly this message of the possibility of transcending the taking form of our human existence. The main witness of this message is Jesus who in the exposure of his total vulnerability broke through the chains of death and found his life by losing it. He challenges us to break through the circle of our imprisonment. He challenges us to face our fellow man without fear and to enter with Him in the fellowship of the weak, knowing that it will not bring destruction but creation, new energy, new life, and—in the end—a new world.

Intimacy and prayer

3

Student-Prayers: Between Confusion and Hope

When we ask about the prayerlife of today's college student we ask to enter into a very intimate world. It is the world where the student faces the ultimate meaning of his existence and tries to relate to what stretches beyond the limits of his birth and death. Entering this world can only happen on invitation. Every form of force will harm this most sensitive area of life and even ruin the same realities which we want to understand.

But why enter at all? Shouldn't this most private domain remain private at all cost? Yet what sounds like respect and protection of a man's individuality might in fact be a fearful avoidance to experience the deepest possible level of human communication. A man who wants to share his prayer wants to share his life, and not just as a sequence of events, emotions and thoughts. He wants to share a moment in which the question of the meaning of existence can be raised. And perhaps it is exactly in the sharing of his prayer that a man is able to reveal his God to his fellow man.

Based on this conviction, some university students asked their friends to write a prayer. There was no sampling in-

41

volved, no systematic selection, no careful divisions into groups, college years or family background. The most simple question was asked: "Are you willing to write a prayer?" The response to this question was the first discovery: "Yes. Yes, I would like to try. Nobody asked me before, but I would like to write a prayer and I will ask my friends too." Friends asked friends and within two months a collection grew of 41 prayers written by students of both sexes, with a wide variety of attitudes and views on life. Some students were used to praying, others never prayed. Some lived with an easy familiarity in the house of God, others wondered if the word "God" made any sense at all. Some took life as a happy selection of good things, others as a torture chamber with closed windows. Some were regular churchgoers, others never went or had stopped going because of boredom or unbelief. But all wrote a prayer and wanted others to read it. And while the collection went from hand to hand, evoking many different reactions, students found themselves reading a prayerbook, which is a rather exceptional kind of book to read on today's college campus.

In this study I would like to present these prayers, not to draw any general conclusion about the religious life of the students, but simply as one of the many witnesses of man's ongoing search for meaning. One of the students who read all the prayers with great care and sensitivity wrote: "A personal prayer falls always, I think, between disciplines or definitions. Something lurks behind the words too personal, too elusive to get at with any system of rigorous analysis. Despite this difficulty a reader can understand and describe what is going on in a particular prayer, and with maturity, sensitivity and attention he may come to understand much of that which lies beneath the words and phrases strung together to make up that prayer."[1] With this same attitude I hope to be able to describe the world of prayer as visible through this collection.

But is there any perspective within which we can place this wide variety of individual expressions? After studying the prayers it seemed that they touched two extreme experiences: the experience of total confusion and self-doubt in which the student finds himself asking for clarity and self-understanding and the experience of a strong and definitive hope, characterized by self-awareness, self-acceptance and the expectance of greater things to come. We find the praying student somewhere between these poles of confusion and hope. So also can we locate in a tentative way the divergent prayers. Taking them together we even can see a movement out of the prison of self-doubt to the freedom of self-confirmation. And moving between these two poles we encounter many Gods, with many faces and many tasks. Most visible in this collection are the following Gods:

1. "The clarifying God"
2. "The banned God"
3. "The big buddy God"
4. "The compassionate God"
5. "The beautiful God"
6. "The giving God"
7. "The coming God"

1. The clarifying God

Under the mask of a self-assertive attitude many students hide deep feelings of confusion. Bombarded by millions of contradicting stimuli, confronted with opposing viewpoints,

---

[1] R. Bradley.

ideals and desires, they often feel lost in the stream of events
and feelings and wonder who they are and where they are
going. Many are persecuted by the question: "Can I do anything meaningful in this mad world, which speaks one day
about nonviolence and the other day about revolution, one
day about a crusade in Europe and the other day about
murder in Vietnam?" In the middle of all this confusion they
have lost track of their ideas, feeling and emotions and have
become entangled in the complexity of their internal life.

When these students pray they are confronted with their
own confusion. "What can I do?" or "What do I want?" is
a question, but a more basic question is "What do I feel?"
And this confusion of mind and cluttering of feelings can
lead to an inability to experience the many differentiations
in life. Joy and sadness, anger and thankfulness, love and
hate seem to blend into a paralyzing lump of unidentifiable
emotions. The result is often apathy, dullness, fatigue. Over-
stimulated, overexposed, overfed with ideals and slogans
stretched in too many different directions, nothing else can
be said than: "I don't care." A dull passivity has become the
only possible attitude. While students are preparing themselves for a great Mardi Gras, one of them prays:

> Well, here we are, another Mardi-Gras weekend—for some a
> time of fun, enjoyment, thoughtfulness and forgetfulness, and
> for some a time of depression and anger.
>
> But for me neither: and that just about sums up the whole
> apathetic slump. It is serious and has gotten to the point where
> its causes—the library, the war, the ugliness, the jokes, the in-
> tolerance—have broken most enthusiasm to the point where
> drifting is the only thing possible.
>
> I don't think that I like drifting—oh, not a rat race, just some
> enthusiasm, some interest, and then I can at least pursue some-
> thing, even though that something may be shaded.
>
> Please help everyone to find enthusiasm and interest.

Out of his dullness and apathy this student asks for articulation and differentiation to find some new handles and directions in the labyrinth of the inner life and rediscover himself within some clear boundaries of identifiable experiences.

This confusion often leads to a very negative self-evaluation. Many students experience vaguely self-contempt, even self-hate. They have lost self-respect and are angry with their own unknown self. You cannot love what you do not know and how can you love yourself, when the only thing you experience is a deep pit of intermingled impulses, feelings, emotions and ideas, of which you are more victim than master. Out of this confusion one student prays:

> Help me find and cherish myself—to solve the problems of myself and others, to more clearly see the direction in which I'm going. It has been so cloudy and jerky—sometimes I wonder if I'm progressing at all—and sometimes I wonder if I can. Remove this doubt I have about myself—or better let me see the doubt and lack of confidence for what it is, and in removing it, learn more of it. I can see in my actions how my doubt and lack of confidence come out. I hide it well, but hiding it makes me worry all the more. Help me remove this self-consciousness which makes me second-guess myself. Let me cease to try to impose a definition on myself, but to act and think naturally. Let me see that all are to be respected, many are to be loved, and some must be fought—and that all men are more than I think they are.

And even praying itself becomes nearly an impossibility. There is so little distance and so much cloudiness that praying creates guilt and enters in the vicious circle of a growing self-devaluation.

> Lord, I don't really feel like praying. I'm confused, everything is confused. I don't know what I'll be doing next year—I don't even know for sure what I want to be doing next year, or what

I should be doing. I feel guilty praying—turning to you at a time like this because I feel two-faced to pray only when I need help and not to pray when I don't.

But somewhere there is a spark of light, hardly noticeable and very subtle. The attitude of praying can sometimes create that little bit of distance which is the beginning of self-knowledge. Praying, if it is anything more than a narcissistic self-complaint, involves someone else, another who is not just me. And in this way we can see that the expression of confusion can become the beginning of its solution. Praying then means creating distance and God's answer is given in the praying act. One student after a long prayer filled with spiritual dizziness and self-doubt writes this short postscriptum:

> This must be a prayer, because it has done something already. As you think about things, they become clearer, and kind of fall into place. I don't think that thinking about problems ever solves any alone, but at least gives a basis for further action and further thought.

Here the clarifying God reveals himself. Here the first step is set out of confusion. Here a road becomes visible and man can at least start to walk on his own feet. New channels of energy become available and the result of this prayer is that a man can feel that he can do something himself. The student's post-script is a beautiful echo of Anton Boisen's conviction: "I do believe in prayer. I believe that its chief function is—to find out what is wanted of us and to enable us to draw upon sources of strength which will make it possible for us to accomplish our task whatever it may be."[2]

---

[2] Anton Boisen, *Out of the Depth* (Harper & Brothers: 1960), p. 111.

Prayer opens our eyes for ourselves and through clarification enables us to step forward in the direction of hope.

2. *The banned God*

Sometimes the step out of confusion means a step away from God. It is not seldom that man found internal rest and harmony once he had the courage to shake off his torturing God. His present Godless life feels like a liberation after years of painful and humiliating occupation. This experience of change is a conversion experience in reverse, but with the same psychological effects: new internal freedom, growing self-respect, new hope. For some students their God-ridden past is filled with memories of scrupulosity, guilt-feelings, fear for punishment, unbearable responsibilities and unlivable expectations. They felt surrounded by a wall of prohibitions and deprived by God's cruel omnipotence, omniscience and omnipresence from their own self-respect. Exposed in their miserable nakedness to God's intruding eye they were like men robbed of their most intimate identity. For these individuals the murder of their God was an experience of conversion, and the way to self-discovery, self-respect, self-awareness and self-affirmation. They had to have the courage to ban their tyranical God and to claim back their own most personal individuality.

Therefore, prayer to a nonexisting God, the banned God, is not an embarrassing joke, but a deep and sincere expression of a paradise gained. Such a prayer can show how thin the edge is between agnosticism and Christian faith. The banning of God has created a new peace of mind and a fearless heart. One student prays:

> When I speak to you I strongly suspect that You aren't "out there" now and never were. I have lost You and I feel better for it because You diminished me and wouldn't let me be

myself. I always felt I had to consider what You wanted me to do, what image or state of perfection You demanded.

Since the time of our separation I've grown more selfish. I'm concerned a lot with myself, with my own development as a human being. I suppose I still want to be perfect, but not for my own sake, nor to please You. What matters now are the others.

This is a real prayer. What makes it a prayer? It is a dialogue, a conversation. That means that here one is not rigid, closed, bitter and cynical, but open to a response, willing to listen and available for growth. It is the same student who prays:

If and when I find You again—and I'm certainly leaving my-self open to that—I just know that I'll find You in the Others and in my Self. Who knows, maybe You are what is best in each of us.

God has become an obstacle in man's desire to be good for his neighbor. Instead of the way to the other, He is in the way. A prayer to such a God becomes an act of cowardice or just weakness. A student painfully aware of the contradiction involved in his praying attitudes describes his conversion from God to men as follows:

There just doesn't seem to be any real reason to pray—I don't say prayers any more. I'm still not really convinced that there is such a thing as a God. You don't achieve or receive anything aside from your own ambitions and work or from another. Thanking people involved in a specific situation seems much more relevant than thanking God.

There is someone more important than God, that is man. God-talk is boring, trivial, fruitless and vicious. It keeps us away from what really matters. With a new found freedom a student says:

I can't be bothered with the trivial things the church worries about. It just seems a waste of time.

In all these prayers, or nonprayers, God is experienced as blocking the way to the self and therefore to the other. The prayer for self-discovery is a prayer asking God to leave, sometimes forcing him to get out of the way in order to find freedom and self. So a man steps out of his confusion by banning a suffocating God from his existence.

3. *The big buddy God*

In a seemingly drastic contrast with the banned God, we encounter in the student-prayers the big-buddy-God. It is the God with whom you can talk with an easy-going familiarity. In a remarkable way God combines the qualities of a playmate and a cure-all. He is like a big-brother, part of the family, but stronger and willing to solve with a friendly smile the worries of the baby-boy. You can speak with him in a shoulder slapping way and brag about him when you need some support in your self-esteem. You can count on Him every moment and you can forget about your own problems, since He is around all the time, never too tired to help out. One prayer to this big-buddy-God reads as follows:

Lord, there are an awful lot of things that bug me lately. The real uncertainty of next year, especially all the people I snub every day—as a result of a lot of stagnant relationships. Really, Lord, I'm a pretty imperfect specimen—basically, Lord, help me to keep trying to love a little bit better and to be a little bit more open to others. Also, Lord, help me to become what You want me to become. Help me to choose the right law school, the right wife, and the right job—make money insignificant—Also remember the guys at home, the guys at school, those getting married and those in Vietnam.

So, Lord, I'm going to play handball now, and I'd like to ask just one more thing of You, that is, help me to live more vibrantly what I believe or at least what I think I believe. Help me to take serious every event in life especially every person, and understand it or him, not condemn it or him. Okay?

P.S. Thanks for dying on the cross for me and my friends.

The casual tone of this prayer is like that of a boy comfortably sitting on daddy's lap. There are many problems, but they don't cut deep, they don't really hurt. They hardly touch the heart of the praying man. If there is confusion, it is confusion of an external nature, which doesn't cause internal turmoil but which can be dealt with by a direct request for help with the unshakable conviction that everything will be okay soon.

This attitude comes close to what William James calls the once-born, healthy-minded type of religion. It is the religion of the man "who's soul is of this sky-blue sort, whose affinities are rather with flowers and birds and all enchanting innocencies than with dark human passions, who can think no ill of man or God, and in whom religious gladness, being in possession from the outset, needs no deliverance from any antecedent burden."[3] William James does not hide his suspicion about this "ultra-optimistic form of the once-born philosophy."[4] He points up the superficial nature of a religion in which all evil is externalized and not recognized as a part of man asking for conversion. This superficiality of the once-born-minded is also obvious in this prayer:

Hey, Big Man. Things are in a sorry state right now. The whole country is in an uproar. You know, I never really thought about it much. I mean in terms of affecting me. Martin Luther King was kind of off in the distance. He was a rabble-rouser. He

---

[3] William James, *The Varieties of Religious Experience* (Enlarged edition. University Books: 1963), p. 80.

[4] *ibid.*, 362.

confronted the people with something new, different and un-
pleasant. It made me stop and think. I don't have any con-
clusions though. I don't imagine You like this mess we've got-
ten ourselves in, but help us out of it, please?

Remarkable here is that the student himself is more or less
aware of his own uninvolvement and aloof distance. But
although he recognizes vaguely his lack of personal responsibility he still expects the solution to come from his big-
buddy-Jesus.

If we analyse both prayers more closely we see that we
can hardly discover any real hope. These prayers are still on
the level of wish-fulfillment. Wishes are concrete; "They
have specific objects and articulate contents."[5] The wish
wants something very specific and belongs more to the surprise level of Santa Claus than to the personalistic level of
faith.

The big-buddy prayers which we quoted are filled with
wishes and expect God to surprise man soon with his great
divine gift. These prayers therefore, are still far away from
self-knowledge, self-acceptance and hope. Although they
seem so opposite from the prayers to the banned God, they
are very close to them when we see them on the continuum
from confusion to hope. This kind of prayers is free from
confusion, but not by facing the problems, but by banning
them or not allowing them to enter into the inner life. The
internal rest of the man who has shaken off the bothersome
God is just as superficial as the relaxed attitude of him who
talks to God as a divine playmate.

---

[5] See Paul Pruyser, "Phenomenology and Dynamics of Hoping,"
Journal for the Scientific Study of Religion 3:86-96 (Fall 1963) and,
A Dynamic Psychology of Religion (Harper & Row: 1968),
pp. 166-170.

4. The compassionate God

In the long row of prayers there is a turning point where a new perspective is breaking through. No entangling confusion nor easy rest, but the beginning of something different pointing to hope, vaguely, hesitantly and tentatively, but clearly recognizably. These prayers can best be called anti-heroic prayers. They ask for a creative passivity in a demanding competitive world.

They are the crying out of a man who uses grades as a measure for success, success as a basis of promotion and promotion as a criterion of human value. They also are a protest against the desires to become a star, to be worshiped for exceptional results, or honored for bravery. They are prayers to a compassionate God, who does not ask for heroic martyrdom, but wants to embrace a weak man.

Father, I ask not that you give me strength nor bravery, nor humility, nor courage. These are but words, straining futilely to compress and to define that which was meant to be open. The more I grasp for these man-made ideas, the more I fail. In the end all words, all exhortations seem little more than hollow clatter. When I listen to these words my life becomes a task, a challenge—and always I fail. Such thinking urges me to "try a little harder." And I fail again. And so on in an endless circular parade both led and followed by proud men.

Perhaps this frustration is your silent voice begging me to stop, to let you carry my "burden." Whenever I do stop, there is no burden. Then I sense your presence in the stillness, a stillness flowing far beneath the sterile incongruency of man alone.

I should ask for nothing, just wait for you to give. But I am impatient and must ask. Father, help me to receive the peace which you constantly offer; help me to hear the frozen stillness of your harmony; help me to be passive; help me to accept; help me to stop.

This sounds like a prayer of an exhausted circus dancer who feels that he can lose balance at any moment and fall from the thin rope in the middle of a roaring crowd. It is the voice of a tired man, tired from the unceasing request to do better, to try harder, to climb higher. It is the cry of a man doubting if he will be able to keep pace with the fast-moving world, and fearful of falling apart under the growing burden of his demanding milieu.

This praying man wants to stop, to surrender in the soft caressing hands of an understanding God, to fall asleep in safe arms, to cry without fear, to let go, relax his tense muscles and rest long and deep, forgetting the cold, cruel and hostile world. In many ways this prayer represents an anticlimax to the banner-waving type of Christianity, in which the brave heroic youth willing to give his life for his commanding God was extolled as an example for all lukewarm believers. It is the other side of the man stimulated and challenged from many pulpits to fight his way through this dangerous world and secure through utmost efforts everlasting rewards in the future-life.

But perhaps we are shortsighted when we only see here a reaction to a triumphalistic past. Perhaps we find here the nucleus of the new mystic, the beginning of a prayer which is not the result of human concentration, but of the emptiness created for the divine Spirit. We can catch a glimpse of this new mysticism when we recognize the new sense of humility shining through the antiheroic prayer. They are smiling prayers, in which man asks for a little bit of happiness, a little bit of beauty, a little bit of meaning in life. One student prays:

I don't want to live in vain—Make me live for something—I'm no hero. I don't really have whatever it is that makes a hero.

But I don't want to be a coward. I don't want to be afraid when the time for courage arrives. Let me do something. Let me do it in my own quiet unheroic way. If I can just be remembered as being a good man, as being a distinct and different man, I will feel that I did not waste my life. If I feel that my living here, that the very fact that I existed and lived on earth, meant something to someone, I will be happy. Let me be remembered by someone. Let me help someone—Don't permit me to just exist as another human being. Make me live. I don't want to live in vain.

The beauty is modesty. The fatigue is less obvious here. The humble desire to be of some good to someone is central. But there very well might have been a purifying experience which made this prayer possible. There is a new rest and freedom not the result of repression or avoidance, but based on the humble recognition of man's important but small place in the face of his Creator.

5. *The beautiful God*

On our way out of confusion we have passed the point where something new was breaking through. In the prayers to the compassionate God we discovered a new openness, a new receptivity which gave room to a creative relationship to the "reality of the unseen" (William James). And although there was still much reaction against the spy-God, the cry for compassion and understanding also meant an opening of the senses for new experiences.

We now come to a group of prayers which can be seen as a dramatic plea for sensitivity. In these prayers students ask to be in touch with what is real, to experience in depth the world which surrounds us and to feel united with the vital sources of life. They look for oneness and a liberation from the painful sense of alienation. They want to touch, taste, smell, hear and see what is beyond their own lonesomeness and surrender to the unspeakable beauty of the divine. They are prayers to the beautiful God, beautiful in a sensual way, in which the analytical distance is broken down in an ecstatic joy making God into a bodily experience. The alienation out of which these prayers are born is most dramatically verbalized by the student who writes:

Alone while in class
Alone with my friends
Alone in a pressing crowd
Where to turn to shelter this all embracing shell?

The world is without life—no longer a friend
The trees sticky leaves, children;
All seem—only unreal.
They out there. I am apart.

Out of this isolation the impulse to dive back into the womb of existence speaks its urging language. These prayers are like prayers of the American Indians who aspired not to be master over the world or to rule creation in God's name but only to merge with nature and experience the participation with the creative forces of life. In their masks the face of man merges with the body of a lizard or snake and in their rituals they hoped to reach the sense of their brotherly place in nature.

This same desire is visible in some of the students who let their hair grow free, dress in a loose unrestrained way, speak about beautiful things and beautiful people and eat the seeds which help them enter in the passive state where colors and sounds embrace them with a tender touch. Central is the desire to step away from the meager emotions of a technocratic society in which superficiality leads to boredom and the breaking of contact with the mysterious powers of reality. And this brings us to a new prayer:

> Help us to see that which is real. A reality. Help us to lie under a tree and enjoy the grass and sky and wind, to have a definitive feeling, perhaps simple, perhaps deep, to think wildly, openly, to stretch.
>
> To hold a hand and mean it, to appreciate beauty, to experience a relationship, a joy, a satisfaction, a sadness, a desperation, an exhaustion. To feel close to an idea, an ideal, and to ourselves. To feel part of a country, a person and the earth. To rise out of the depths of desperation and self-made alienation, and to be close once again to you. These are what we can grasp, these are real. These are experiences. That is our prayer, Lord. To be aware, to rise up, to realize, to understand and to care.

Perhaps more than any of the others this prayer expresses one of the deepest desires of the contemporary student faced with a dismembered and broken reality in which he has to find his place, but which often seems more threatening than inviting. In a milieu that tries to refine the senses through ingenuous instruments, the student wonders if he can trust his own body and if his senses are able to bring him in contact with the reality in which he lives. But as soon as the touch of sensitivity dawns upon him a new vibration pervades him. A girl prays:

> Just to hear . . . the annoying buzz of haunting alarm clocks through the thin walls of those who live nearby.
>
> Just to see . . . a friend who has waited to walk with me over to class, and that look on his face when I've done it again, but I don't know what.
>
> Just to smell . . . the freshness of a spring morning when the sun is warm and winter has passed: when the flowers are budding and the grass is moist.

Just to feel . . . the refreshment of an afternoon shower; the softness of a baby duck; the sand between my toes; the thrill of a tender kiss.

Just to taste . . . not only a snack or a meal, but the sweet and bitter of life; and to love with my entirety the who that they are, whether ugly or gracious or right or sad.

Students like this girl are filled with the experience of new life, new beauty and new energy. They say "Yes" to all that is, and in their humble recognition of their own fragility they open themselves to the splendor of their beautiful God. A new ray of hope is coming through.

6. *The giving God*

The antiheroic prayers showed a first hesitant appreciation of the little things. In the prayers to the compassionate God, a creative passivity became visible and the last two prayers revealed the deep desire to merge with the beautiful God and to experience a new sense of unity and belonging. We are far away from the confused state of mind, with which we started this analysis, but still not arrived at what we can call Christian hope.

The plea for sensitivity with the desire to feel deeply embedded in reality was still in many ways a plea of the lonesome, somewhat isolated man. The need to merge, to be one, to belong, often reveals a regressive impulse, which cannot tolerate the distinction between the praying man and his world, between himself and the other, between his weakness and God's strength. Often it seems as if the quest for belonging means a fear of being different and an unwillingness to claim the individuality of the self. The identity of the praying person, therefore, has not yet a clear form and a prayer for sensitivity can sound somewhat preoccupied. Its God is more a protective device than the giving other.

Obviously we only speak about differences in degree, but in the prayers to the beautiful God, God is hardly recognized as the other who is free to give or not to give. He is more an indispensable source of warmth always available to offer comfort. But once God is recognized as the other who gives in freedom, man is able to think. Sensitivity is a condition to experience God's gifts, but thanks includes also the willingness to recognize the distance between the giver and the receiver.

When man is able to thank he is able to know his limitations without feeling defensive and to be self-confident without being proud. He claims his own powers and at the same time he confesses his need for help. Thanking in a real sense avoids submissiveness as well as possessiveness. It is the act of a free man who can say: I thank you. Here I and you are two different persons with different identities who can enter in an intimate relationship without losing their own selves. An act of free thanking requires a careful balance between closeness and distance. Too much closeness can lead to a self-effacing dependency, too much distance to an overevaluation of the self with a defensive pride.

Many of the student prayers are so self-centered, so full of deep personal concern, or so craving for sympathy and protection that there is not enough distance to say thanks. But there are exceptions in which a new freedom is visible and a prayer becomes a hymn of thanksgiving.

Lord, thank You for life, love and people.

Dear Lord, thank You for the beautiful day, for the flowers, for the birds, for my family, for my friends, for me.

for all that has been—thanks
for all that will be—yes!

In thanks man is open and moves outward. In confusion all the attention is drawn inward in an attempt to unravel the complexities of the internal world, hardly leaving any possibility to say thanks. In confusion man clings to himself, in thanks he stretches out his hands and points to the source of new energy, new life, new love. Thanks then can even become possible in a sad world. One student concludes a long prayer with the words:

> What can I say but thank You; in the middle of bad it has never been so good.

Here thanks can shake off the depression of the present and make hope a possibility.

7. *The coming God*

When many students were asked to read the prayers and to give their reactions to them there was an almost unanimous attraction to one prayer which we consider a prayer to the coming God. Although different students could sympathize with many strong positive or negative affects, expressed in the collection, the attitude communicated through form and content by this prayer called "hope" was immediately recognized as the most desirable, most modern and most Christian.

> I hope that I will always be for each man what he needs me to be.
>
> I hope that each man's death will always diminish me, but that fear of my own will never diminish my joy of life.
>
> I hope that my love for those whom I like will never lessen my love for those whom I do not.
>
> I hope that another man's love for me never be a measure of my love for him.

I hope that every man will accept me as I am, but that I never will.

I hope that I will always ask for forgiveness from others, but will never need be asked for my own.

I hope that I will find a woman to love, but that I will never seek one.

I hope that I will always recognize my limitations, but that I will construct none.

I hope that loving will always be my goal, but that love will never be my idol.

I hope that every man will always have hope.

Here we find ourselves as far away as possible from confusion. Here we listen to a man who stands on solid ground and points into the future. He knows where he is and looks with expectation towards the things to come. The structure and thought of this prayer show a great self-confidence carefully integrated with a deep sense of humility. The prayer illustrates in a beautiful way some of the basic dynamics of the attitude of the mature Christian.

In comparison with the painful self-preoccupation, which we found in the prayer of the confused student, we see here a great sense of self-awareness, self-acceptance. There are clear, but not rigid lines which mark the personality. In this attitude of hope we see a man well defined but always available for redefinition. In comparison with the prayers to the banned God, there is no artificial rest created by a negative conversion but a free dialogue without need to defend. In hope God is no obstacle, but the way to human love. In comparison with the prayers to the big-buddy-God, there is no easy optimism nor simplistic wish-fulfilling thinking. The hope expressed is on a very personal level and never con-

cretized in toy-like desires. Man does not ask the coming
God for favors, but opens himself to a deepening of an interpersonal relationship, which depends on two persons, and
can never be forced. In comparison with the antiheroic
prayers to the compassionate God, there is no feeling of
fatigue or reaction against an overdemanding society. In
hope man does not react to a frustrating past, but reaches
forward to a promising future. In comparison with the
prayers to the beautiful God, the praying man here is less
alienated and more self-composed. There is no desire to
merge with God, but to strengthen the own identity. In hope
man does not ask to vanish and lose himself in the embracing arms of a protecting God, but he experiences his being
different as a creative possibility. In comparison with the
prayers to the giving God, thanks is less explicitly formulated, but constantly presupposed. Real hope is impossible
without the deep awareness that life is a gift and holds endless promises.

So we see in the prayer to the coming God the attitude
of hope as an attitude of self-awareness and self-acceptance
from which man enters in a creative dialogue with his living God, constantly leaving behind his past and stretching
forward to a future which he experiences as an inexhaustible source of new life.

We tried to enter into the intimacy of the student prayerlife. We did this on invitation by studying the prayers written
by the student himself and offered for evaluation. By seeing
the whole collection as a move out of confusion towards ma-

ture hope we wanted to prevent ourselves from labeling the different student prayers as more or less "good" or "bad." We only wanted to understand where the student could be located in his search for meaning and a God whom he can call his God. The distinctions between the different God's were perhaps too artificial, but they were intended to make it easier to recognize the intimate moves of man to come closer to himself and the God of his faith.

4

Pentecostalism on Campus

Since the Pentecostal movement has become a vivid reality on some university campuses, many active participants, as well as distant observers, have asked, "Is this healthy or dangerous, something to be encouraged or something to be avoided?"

Various students who experienced the gift of tongues, who felt the Real Presence of the Holy Spirit and for whom a new world of feelings has opened itself, expressed their change: "It is a tremendous experience. It is new, unique, full of joy and peace. I am different, that is for sure. Only one who has surrendered can really understand what I am talking about. Many problems I have long been struggling with just seemed to vanish, became like an empty shell falling off. Heavy burdens became feather-light things; hostile attitudes converted to deep sympathy. People whom I once feared are now my friends. Those whom I hated I can love, those who were masters are partners. I know with a deep certainty that God has spoken to me in a new way."

But sometimes the same students will tell you the other side of their feelings: "I wonder if it is all real, if it is really me. It is like another world which is not mine; one so overwhelming that it seems unreal. Once in a while, after a prayer meeting when I am by myself, I feel lonesome and depressed. Will it last? Perhaps it is just for a short time and then my problems will come back. I wonder if it is really good for me."

The same ambivalence is expressed by outsiders. They see people pray, sing, and read together; they see their happiness, joy and new convictions; but they wonder how real or healthy it is. And since this is all so close, it seems very difficult to find the distance to understand without falling into a fanatic rejection and ridicule on the one hand or an uncritical enthusiasm on the other.

This essay is an attempt to clarify certain issues and to be of some help in an honest evaluation. I will use, besides my own observations and discussions with students, the study by Kilian McDonnell, O.S.B., "The Ecumenical Significance of the Pentecostal Movement."[1] I will approach the subject from three perspectives.

A *historical perspective*

Although Pentecostalism was originally found among people with a low economic status and closely related with the nonliturgical churches (such as the Assembly of God Church), since 1955 a new wave of Pentecostalism has entered the more prosperous communities, inspired many intellectuals, and established itself in such liturgical churches as the Lutheran and Episcopalian.

McDonnell, who studies the rising Pentecostalism with a group of anthropologists, is probably the most informed and knowledgeable theologian in this area. Considering it as "the fastest growing movement within the Christian tradition"[2] he asks himself, "How can the Pentecostals with so few

---

[1] Kilian McDonnell, O.S.B. "The Ecumenical Significance of the Pentecostal Movement" (*Worship*, December 1966).

[2] *ibid.*, p. 609.

means form such apostolic Christians while our liturgies rich in theological content and tradition fail to communicate the urgency of evangelization to the faithful?" Do our liturgies develop a sense of community? Do they form a congregation which acts, prays, listens, sings and sorrows together, a true community of the redeemed? Have the Roman Catholics become comfortable with the too-oft-extolled beauties of the Roman Liturgy (sobriety, grandeur, clarity, objectivity, lapidary formulations, fixity of form, supranational appeal—the list reads as though drawn up by an enemy) and failed to notice that, in every liturgical instance and in every cultural context, sobriety and objectivity may not be virtues to emphasize, that grandeur amidst poverty may be an indictment, that supranational appeal may, in fact, be a species of Roman liturgical colonialism?

Pentecostals are in many lands the fastest-growing Christian denomination. Why? "Undoubtedly the answer involves many factors, but this much we know. Our liturgies have failed."[3] And McDonnell even wonders whether "St. Paul would not feel more at home in the free fervor of a Pentecostal meeting than in the organized dullness of our liturgical celebrations."[4] There is no doubt about one thing. The rapidly growing interest in the Pentecostal prayer meeting at university-campus reveals an intensive need, a long-hidden frustration which manifests itself in the sudden breakthrough of a form of behavior which is rather unusual in a student-community.

It is difficult to imagine how a Catholic university looked in the twenties and thirties. About the University of Notre Dame, where John F. O'Hara was the prefect of religion,

---

[3] *ibid.*, pp. 622-623.

[4] *ibid.*, p. 615.

Joe Hoffman writes: "O'Hara gave Notre Dame its enormous standing within the Catholic populace of the United States as a place where the solid practice of Catholicism could be found. His goals were clear-cut and defined: Mass, Communion, frequent confession, devotion to the Blessed Sacrament and to Mary. His methods were novenas in preparation for Christmas, Easter, Mother's Day, and exams. There were processions, hours of adoration, the rosary, first Friday devotions, and all of them were popular. Freshmen arriving on campus were immediately indoctrinated into the system. By means of the Religious Bulletin, which was read as much beyond the campus as by the students, O'Hara hammered at students foibles, suggested means for advancing in the spiritual life, gave timely notice of approaching religious events, commented on the spiritual significance of the news of the day, presented points of character development, gave short instructions on ideals, corrected student abuses, and answered difficulties. It was spiritual reading in tabloid form. O'Hara kept statistics on religious practice, published religious surveys and was keenly aware of the tempo and mentality of the student body. He was extremely successful."[5]

Today the picture is completely different. A university is no longer a place with easygoing students who consider their four years as a relatively relaxed time with abundant opportunity for prayer, sports, social life and extracurricular activities; rather, it is a very ambitious and competitive institution. Today, students often look upon their four years as a race in which only the fittest survive. In the educational revolution of the post-Sputnik era, academic excellence became the key word.

---

[5] Joseph Hoffman, C.S.C., unpublished article.

But competition demands a price. Most students take the challenge and are able to utilize the new pressures in a useful and often creative way. But many do not, and instead they often develop an excessive amount of anxiety and tension and experience a painful lonesomeness which they hide beneath the surface of seemingly well-adjusted behavior. The university community now counts hundreds of very lonesome men who consider their neighbors more as rivals than as friends. For many, their roommate is a stranger and their classmate a threat. "Everyone for himself, and God for us all." That seems most safe. Knowledge becomes a weapon by which you stay in school, avoid the Army, win a fellowship, and make a career. And the Church does not seem to help very much. Going through a time of reevaluation and extreme self-criticism, she offers more questions than answers. Instead of a safe home, she is more a source of deep discomfort for a man who looks for a solid support in a tumbling world.

In this context the Pentecostal movement very well can be understood as a revival, a rekindling of the devotional Church, or the revenge of a repressed sentiment. Everyone who enters a Pentecostal meeting is suddenly confronted with all that seems to be at odds with a "typical" university student. In the midst of the congregation, students witness how their lonesomeness and insecurity have been overcome by the gift of the Holy Spirit. One who never had a friend and always felt afraid now feels free to share his deepest thoughts and desires with his fellow man. Long struggles with most embarrassing problems are wiped away by the infusion of God's Spirit. Sadness is changed to joy, restlessness to peace, despair to inner content, and separation to togetherness.

On a campus where people stay relatively distant from each other, the most intimate ideas are shared and the barriers to communication are broken. Where men hardly touch each other, they embrace and hold each other in a free physical contact. They lay hands on each other's shoulders and heads, pray aloud for each other's needs, and let themselves be led by deep spiritual impulses to which they surrender in ecstatic joy and happiness. The new feelings are so great and overpowering that they cannot be caught in human concepts or words, but break through in ecstatic sounds varying in tone and intensity and expressing a prayer of total surrender and praise, saying with Jeremiah, "Ah, Lord, I don't know how to speak." Hands, eyes and mouth express unknown happiness, openness and joy. Young men move up and down in the pleasant rhythm of biblical songs, or are quiet in a long and contemplative silence. So intense is the exchange that many feel a new, warm intensity pervading their whole persons. Their hands radiate new power and a soft and tender breeze touches their skins. Joy and happiness may break through in tears and sweat and the intensity of the prayer may lead to a happy and satisfying experience of physical exhaustion caused by total surrender.

The Spirit has come. He who asks will receive and feel that God is not a strange God. He will taste again His sweetness, hear His internal call, and be able to love Him with his whole person, body and soul, without any reservation.

A psychological perspective

How can we evaluate this new movement? We can understand it as a revival of the devotional Church and as a reaction of a repressed religious sentiment in a cool and competitive world. But is it healthy or sick? Does it cure or make wounds? It is very difficult to give an outright answer, but perhaps some considerations may be of help.

Does it heal or hurt? There is no doubt that many people who surrendered to this experience get a tremendous and often very sudden relief from their mental and spiritual pains. Problems they have been struggling with for years are wiped away in a moment and lose their unbearable weight. The questions are: Are they cured or covered? Is the real human conflict resolved or "snowed under" by the overwhelming power of a new experience?

We know that electroshock, an artificially induced emotional experience, can cover a depression for many years but does not cure it. It may make us forget our problems for some years, but, in fact, it delays the process of cure by not using the human qualities to heal. One might wonder if the miraculous effect of the Pentecostal experience is not in a certain way like a shock treatment. If a young man or woman suddenly feels redeemed from deep mental suffering, they might, in fact, paralyze their internal human ability to overcome their problem, and when the pains recur later on they might be more discouraged than before.

If we use sleeping pills, we certainly will fall asleep but, at the same time, we can kill our own capacities to find physical rest and become quite dependent on these external forces. And, if the Pentecostal experience in many cases gives this sudden freedom, sudden friendship, sudden happiness and joy, we might prevent the gradual development of our internal capacities to develop meaningful, lasting friendships, to enjoy happiness, and to tolerate frustrations. Many people who have had deep, internal religious experiences (during retreats, cursillos, novitiates, etc.) all can witness to the fact that they relieved many pains for a while, but that the real test came later when there were no feelings to depend on, no experiences to count on. The task lies in the desert where God is not feelable and naked faith is all we have.

The Pentecostal experience might take away (even permanently) certain real problems, but it is very doubtful that it will cure deep mental suffering. It might only cover it up and delay the attempt for a real cure.

Can it be dangerous? For many people, perhaps even for most, it hardly seems to be dangerous. It might be even beneficial to a certain extent, especially for those who through retreats, cursillos and other religious practices have become exposed to the inner feelings that are in line with the Pentecostal experience. But for some it is dangerous —very dangerous.

First of all, for those who are not prepared, every inducement of a strong emotion can break and do serious harm. The Christian tradition has been deeply convinced of the importance of preparation. Christ did not come to this world before a long preparation of His people. We do not celebrate Christmas without Advent, nor Easter without Lent. And St. Paul distinguishes between Christians who still need spiritual milk and those who are ready for solid food. The whole mystical tradition stresses the need for purification in order to enter into intimacy with God and the danger of unprepared exposure to divine powers.

Several students showed remarkable signs of anxiety and confusion. They were so overwhelmed by these new feelings that they lost their hold on reality. They found they could no longer study nor concentrate on their daily work; they felt a pushing urge to share with others. In some cases, physical and mental exhaustion were visible, and people felt on the edge of a physical or mental breakdown. This is dangerous and may lead to psychotic reaction, which needs hospitalization and special psychiatric help in order to be cured. These are exceptional cases, but still no less a source of concern.

Secondly, there are those who strongly desire to have the gifts of the Spirit but do not feel able to come to the real experience. They wonder why others are so happy, and they are not; why others can speak in tongues and they cannot; why others feel free to embrace each other, and they do not. More than ever before, they feel like outsiders or even outcasts. And they wonder, "What is wrong with me that I do not receive the gifts?" Feelings of guilt and depression can result from this, and many may feel more lonesome than before. For those who ask but do not receive, the Pentecostal movement can create real dangers.

There is a heavy responsibility on the leaders of the movement. Emotion, and certainly religious emotions, need careful direction, careful guidance, and careful care.

Does it create community? Who could deny this? The free and easy way in which the participants relate to each other, talk, sing and pray together should convince everybody that here a real, new community is formed. Still there are some questions here. By suddenly breaking through the barriers of shyness and distance, many have given away their privacy. Many have shown their deepest self to their fellow man and laid themselves open for the other. They have stripped themselves of their reservations and inhibitions and have shared their most intimate feelings, ideas and thoughts with others. In a way they have merged their personality with their friends and given up their otherness.

But, is this real community? One who has given away so much of himself creates an unquenchable need to be constantly together with the other to whom he has given himself, in order to feel a whole person. Many students who actively participated in the prayer meetings felt terribly lonesome during the vacation and felt a deep urge and desire to be with their friends again. Instead of creating the freedom to leave the group and to go out and work, many want to remain in the safe protection of the togetherness where they can really feel at home.

The lack of distance and the stress on intimacy make the creative community hardly possible. A good liturgy always should be characterized by a subtle balance between closeness and distance. It should offer different modes and levels of participation and many ways of religious experience. Perhaps it seldom did before and is only thought of as a distant, cool reality. But in the Pentecostal movement on campus, closeness has become so central that there is little room left for those who want to retain some distance and keep an intimacy for themselves.

In this context the danger is real that the Pentecostal movement creates a situation in which there is a growing desire to reinforce the feelings of oneness and togetherness, which makes the community highly self-centered and hinders the development of the autonomous Christian who does not depend on the other to feel his own commitments. A real community is for stretching out. The Pentecostal community tends to be bent over inwards, and, without so wanting or aspiring, to become an in-group, developing the idea of a spiritual elite (as the cursillo did) with a subtle handling of the terms "we" and "they."

Are the prayer meetings all spontaneous? The informal, somewhat casual character of the Pentecostal meetings suggests that the real leadership is given to the Holy Spirit. But on closer observation, the meetings are found to be much more organized. There is a certain program that reappears in most Pentecostal meetings: First, witnesses, songs, readings, which prepare for the baptism of the Spirit. Then there is some time allotted for free conversation in which people share their experiences. Finally, after offering more prayers, songs and readings, the laying on of the hands takes place, leading to a climax in the speaking in tongues and the praising of the Lord in ecstatic forms of happiness and joy. This all could not take place without strong and very influential leaders.

But here a new question arises. Who accepts responsibility or authority? The "leaders" refer immediately to the Spirit as the great leader. To the question "Can't the experience be very dangerous for some people?" they would reply, "The Holy Spirit cannot do dangerous things. He is a healing force." In this way the "leaders" refuse explicit leadership, responsibility and authority, confiding in the immediate intervention of God. But in so doing they tend to neglect a definite responsibility, not only in terms of preparation and the actual event but also in terms of the long-range consequences that these experiences will have on the ongoing development of the spiritual life of the people involved.

A *theological perspective*

An active participant of the Pentecostal movement will probably pay very little attention to a psychological approach to his experience. He might even feel psychology to be a hindrance to the free movements of the Spirit.

But this immediately raises the question of the theological significance of the Pentecostal movement. Most remarkable is the conviction of the immediate intervention of the Holy

Spirit in human life. During the meetings the "leaders" often explain how he who is willing to surrender and ask for God's coming will experience the eruption of the Spirit in this human world and allow Him to take over the initiative. "Pentecostalism was, and to a degree remains, more a movement than a church," McDonnell has said.[6] We cannot speak about a Pentecostal doctrine, and perhaps it is for this reason that Pentecostalism so easily becomes a part of different religious institutions to which it adapts itself quite easily. For entering the Catholic Church, Pentecostalism could establish contact at the sacramental level by showing "the relation of the sacramental life to personal holiness and practical piety."[7]

It is, therefore, understandable that Pentecostalism brings people back to their religious practices. Often students who did not "practice their religion" return to confession, Communion, and their lost devotion to Our Lady and the rosary. In no way does Pentecostalism seem to threaten the Catholic orthodoxy. The opposite seems true. In the eyes of many, it seems to point to a reinforcing of the basic Roman Catholic doctrines and beliefs.

But it is exactly here where many theologians raise questions. For, while not denying any Catholic doctrine or practice, the Pentecostals within the Catholic Church act in a way which does not take into account the major development of the recent renewal in Catholic theology. A deeper understanding of the incarnation leads to a rethinking of the humanity of God. More and more it has become clear that God reveals Himself to man through man and his world

---

[6] Kilian McDonnell, O.S.B., *op. cit.*, p. 623.

[7] *ibid.*, p. 621.

and that a deeper understanding of human behavior leads us to a deeper understanding of God. The new insights of psychology, sociology, anthropology and so forth are no longer feared as possible threats to the supernatural God, but more as an invitation to theological reflection on the new insights and understandings. Vatican II strongly supported this humanization of the Church, and the new theology was a great encouragement to mobilize all the human potentialities in the different levels of human life as being the most authentic way to understand the voice of God to His people. The new theology was "discovered" by a deeper understanding of the createdness of the world, by discerning that there is a task of Christian secularization. It was exactly this that the first Christians did: demythologize Caesar and the State. The more we make the world what it ought to be, a created reality with tremendous potentialities for growth, the more this world calls for Him, who is Uncreated. And in this sense secularization is possible only by faith.

In the perspective of this trend in theology, which also encourages more social action and "worldly" involvement, the Pentecostal trend seems a step back. It calls for God's immediate intercession outside the human potentials. In a way it seems that God does not use man, unless as a passive instrument which is the victim of the struggle between demonic and divine forces. The devil is an alien power invading man, and so is the Spirit. The question then becomes, "Who is possessing me?" But possession, good or evil, remains a passive state; it does not give full credit to the basic Christian idea that we are created to create, and to realize our deepest human potentialities in the service of our fellow men, in the love of whom we discover the Spirit of God.

Having discussed the Pentecostal movement as a revival of the devotional Church, as a religious reaction to a world with a heavy stress on achievement, and as raising many psychological and theological questions, the critical tone might have overshadowed a deeper concern about a valid religious experience. We might have overlooked that in one way the Pentecostal movement is an invitation to a deeper search. It made God a living God, a real experience, an actual event. Whereas the whole field of theological education is desperately looking for ways to bring theology from "brain level to guts level," the Pentecostals certainly do it. And it is no surprise that many envy those who experience the presence of God as an undeniable reality. Is it not just this that all the forms of renewal (liturgical, social, clerical, etc.) are trying to do—to make religious life something vibrant, a living source of constant inspiration?

The new wave of Pentecostalism on campus obviously answers a burning need in many students. It worries many who are concerned about the effects on the mental health of some of the participants, it places a heavy responsibility on the leaders of the movement, and it disturbs many theologians; but it also offers a chance to come to a new realization of the crucial importance of valid religious experience as an authentic part of the Christian life. It would be a pity if we missed this chance by a hasty judgment and an intolerant condemnation.

Intimacy and
community

5

Depression in the Seminary

It is not too long ago that the stereotype of the seminarian offered the picture of a very nice, sweet boy, somewhat talkative, easily excited about such innocent things as a recent article, naive, inexperienced especially in matters of sex, but always good-natured, friendly, smiling, and ready to help even when not asked.

That stereotype is changing rapidly. What we see today is far from an easy-going, optimistic young man. We are struck by quite different characteristics. We are more likely to find a problem-ridden, struggling student who takes himself, his world and his future very seriously, who wants to debate and discuss many issues, who is seldom relaxed, but inclined to experience his youth as a long and dark tunnel the end of which he does not see.

And whereas we tended to think of the seminary as a place with joyful, self-confident people, now a visitor might find it to be a place with troubled, doubting people, pervaded with a general atmosphere of depression. Although we are stereotyping and therefore simplifying, we cannot avoid the growing conviction that depression is one of the most surprising symptoms in our seminary communities. If it is true that depression is considered as one of the main problems of the college student, this is even more the case if we consider the seminarian of today. For not only a distant look but even many intensive discussions with seminarians leave one with the feeling that a heavy cloud, undefined and mysterious, is darkening the life of the seminary.

And many staff members find themselves amazed and deeply disappointed when they discover that after years of conscious modernization and liberalization, after many efforts to open a closed system to free an unfree institution, they find their students sad instead of happy, unfriendly and moody instead of good-natured, closed and suspicious instead of open and communicative. This seemingly strange phenomenon demands our special attention today. Our main question is: What is the relationship between formation and depression? And, as no clinician will ever advise any therapeutic measure without a careful and specific diagnosis, we will first try to understand the nature of the depression and its correlation with different new techniques in formation. Then we will try to make some suggestions which might help us in our task to overcome this painful and often destructive symptom.

I. Diagnostic Considerations

There is no doubt that we who are seminary staff members find ourselves in a very complex situation, actually in the middle of a paradox. We are giving to people who come to us for formation the freedom to educate themselves. We are taking away structures from people who want to be formed through channeling their unstructured drives. We have become deeply convinced that the highly regimented seminary life belongs definitely to the past, but also we have discovered that many new freedoms do not always give the desired satisfaction. In this context we have to face the problem of seminary depression.

I propose to discuss this problem in two ways: as a problem of identity for the students and staff, and as a problem of new educational methods.

A. *Depression as an identity problem*

1. A problem of student identity.

Staff-members are dealing with students who realize that they have not yet fully developed their potentialities, who experience a tremendous amount of energy, and who have only a vague idea in which direction they want to go. The students all hope to find three things:

a) Competence, which enables them to cope with the demands of society.

b) Control, which provides them with channels for their unruly impulses.

c) Vocation, which gives them the conviction that they are called to do what they felt vaguely attracted to.

Some will discover that they are not intelligent enough to become competent, some will find that their deepest desires point in a direction other than celibate community life, and many will recognize that they are not called for the work they felt inclined to in the beginning. But it is certain that all are looking for a structure, clear, explicit and articulated, in which they can test themselves and be tested by others in order to allow the necessary decisions for their future life. If this is true we immediately become aware of a severe identity crisis in terms of competence, impulse control and vocation.

a) If a seminarian wants competence he finds himself involved in one of the most difficult fields to feel competent in

—theology. The questions of theology vary from questions regarding specific issues all the way to the question of whether theology is a field for study at all. Very few students feel proud of theology as their discipline in the way a lawyer, doctor, sociologist, or psychologist is proud of his field, and most often they hope to become competent in other areas of study besides theology in order to feel like valuable members of society.

b) If a seminarian wants to find control for his strong drives and impulses, he finds himself in a situation where many taboos are questioned and in which he finds many ambiguous signals regarding the expression of his erotic desires. What has vanished is clarity. A student who pronounced temporary vows and dates a girl on the side is not expelled from the seminary, but rather it is suggested to him in many ways that it might be good to have some dating experience before he makes up his mind. Not too long ago the so-called "particular friendships" were a subject of concern to many faculty members, and of ridicule to the students who did not really know what their superiors were so concerned about. But today the staff has become afraid to even warn against particular friendships whereas many students find themselves in energy-devouring personal relationships with roommates or friends and are sometimes made very anxious due to the obvious sexual feelings which have come to their awareness. Overt homosexual relations which ten years ago were mostly a part of the fantasy of the staff now at times have become a part of the student's problems.

c) If a student comes to deepen his vocation, he finds that hardly anybody can tell him what it means to be a priest. We might even say that the closer he comes to ordination the vaguer his ideas about the priesthood become. When he entered the seminary, he perhaps wanted to be a man like his uncle-priest, his teacher-priest, or like one of the priests he admired, but while going through the years of formation he is exposed to so much questioning, doubting and personal failures that he starts wondering more and more if he should give the most explicit unchangeable commitment to the most undefined and unclear profession. At the same time he wonders who is calling whom. Ten years ago it was clear that the church called and that it was an honor, privilege and election to be ordained to the priesthood. The representatives of the church made it clear: "If you don't live up to the expectations, we ask you to leave." But now the student seems to say to the church: "If you don't live up to my expectations I am leaving." And in many subtle ways it is communicated to the student that nobody wants to lose him and that he can make more demands on the church than the church on him. And although it might seem that this form of student power is attractive to the seminarian, the fact of the matter is that nobody wants to enter a profession which does not contain a demanding call.

So we see that precisely in the three main areas of seminary formation, Competence, Control and Vocation, the student feels frustrated. He feels like a man without a respected discipline, surrounded by ambiguous signals concerning his impulse control and preparing himself for a vocation which has become subject to endless questioning. Slowly the idea crawls up to him that the most unpopular thing to do these days is to become a priest. For a young man, full of energy, ambition and generosity, commitment to an unappreciated, nonchallenging and unclear life seems no commitment at all. And it is not difficult to see that this identity crisis can become the source of a painful depression.

2. A problem of staff identity.

The problem, however, is not just a student problem. The new attitudes of the faculty also explain part of this strange feeling of a collective depression. In a somewhat complicated and seldom recognized way, the democratization of student-faculty relations cause unexpected conflicts. Not too long ago seminaries were places with many rules, usually strict observance and a clear-cut division of authority. There was a lot of rebellion and anger caused by this structure, but students knew to whom to show their anger and against whom to rebel. There was usually a clear system of reward and punishment and students knew what to expect when they took a risk and were caught in the act—frequently a very innocent act of trespassing some quite irrelevant rule. But then someone came to them and said: "It is up to you, if you want to go to Mass or not, if you want to stay in bed or not, go to parties or not, date girls or not, stay up all night or not, come to the recreation or not. You know what you are supposed to do. It is up to your own conscience to do it." Most good, willing and idealistic staff members don't always see what this means. Many times it simply means, "We expect you to do all these things and follow all these rules, but we will not enforce them. We trust you and your own judgment. We hope you won't disappoint us."

The result of this new attitude is the situation of sin without the possibility of doing penance. Seminarians now act in many ways which they know that their superiors don't like, but nobody says anything, nobody objects, reprimands or punishes. They only look disappointed, personally offended, and are saying with their eyes: "I thought I could trust you, but now you do this to me." If a man has nobody to punish him when he feels he deserves it, he starts punishing himself. It is this inward-turned hostility which causes the depression which has become such a pervasive mood in many seminarians. And many staff members are surprised and even bitterly disappointed that all their generous gifts of freedom to the students are not accepted with a joyful thanks, but result in an often loaded and chokingly unfree student-staff relationship. We should take a closer look at this phenomenon. Two aspects seem important: a) The personalized punishment, and b) The verbal and nonverbal communication of doubts.

a. The personalized punishment

The staff very often is disappointed that the students don't live up to the expectations. Students prove less generous than the faculty hoped. They take advantage of their new freedom, do not express thanks for it, but only ask for more. Superiors and other faculty members very often feel personally hurt, and although their hands are itching to slap the student in the face, they feel too liberal to do so, and have to resort to a very subtle and often harmful form of punishment, such as: speaking about lack of trust, sudden inappropriate anger about very small things, looking somber and heavy, and communicating on a very personal level that they are offended and that the students make their life miserable. And just as no child can adequately react to his mother who instead of punishing the child for breaking a glass, says, "Don't you love mama more than to do this to me?", so a student does not know how to handle this highly personalized form of punishment. He can only feel guilty and unable to do anything about it. And that is what creates this tense and choking feeling which takes the humor out of relationships and makes everyone hypersensitive to each other.

b. Communication of doubts

The second aspect of the student-staff relationship which can lead to depression is the way in which the staff communicates its own problems. Many faculty members are questioning the same basic values the students are questioning. They realize that the student problems are not just problems related to their own individual growing pains, but to the growing pains of the whole church. And many seminary teachers are doubting if it is good to encourage a young, intelligent man to become a priest in a community full of confusion and worries. They are asking themselves: "Am I really making a man happy by encouraging him to persevere in the seminary? Can I really give a meaningful answer to his question of what it means to be a priest in a modern world? Does it really make sense to advise him to commit himself for life to a status in which sexual intimacy cannot be striven for? Can I take the responsibility, even when it is a partial responsibility, for anybody's choice of a profession which is in the middle of drastic change?"

These doubts and this anguish do not remain unnoticed by students. In many verbal and nonverbal ways these existential questions enter into the student-faculty relationship. Identification is still the main process by which a man finds his vocation in life. Strong convincing personalities, who give an attractive visibility to their way of life, are the most powerful influences on a young man's life choice. Who wants to become a doctor when his teachers don't believe that they can cure, who wants to be coached by a coach who does not believe that he can win a game, who wants to become a teacher when his professor is only bitter about his students? And who wants to become a priest if he lives with priests who question the foundations of their commitment: the nature of the priesthood, the church, the incarnation and the concept of God. And although these questions are not always personal questions, they are so much a part of the general atmosphere of religious life today that only a stubborn isolationist can completely stay away from them.

Therefore we might wonder if many faculty members who encourage their students to discuss their problems in an open exchange of ideas and adopt the role of understanding listeners themselves, do not in fact, although not intentionally, pass on their burden. And students might experience this as if they are told: "You might like to have a try at the problems which we did not find an answer for ourselves." It might even be possible that many forms of liberalization in today's seminary formation are felt by the students to be testimony of the incapacity to offer meaningful structures on the side of the staff. Many seminarians, who have participated in year-long discussions on about every possible basic subject are showing signs of fatigue, disappointment, confusion and even hostility. Some even feel cheated, as if they had wasted their time groping with questions which don't lead anywhere and are doomed to create frustration.

And so we find not only depression related to the identity crisis of the students but also related to the identity crisis of the staff. It is exactly the mutual reinforcement of many doubts, uncertainties and worries which makes it so difficult to lift the hovering cloud above the seminary. If we now will try to analyze some of the new trends in seminary formation we have to try to understand the temptation of creating a vicious circle of depression which is very difficult to break.

B. Depression and the new educational methods

Having discussed the seminary depression as a problem of identity of students as well as staff members, we now should have a closer look at some new educational techniques to explore their possible relationships with this phenomenon. We will limit our discussion to two new approaches in seminary education which have become very popular in practically all modern seminaries in the United States as well as in Europe: I will call them dialogue and small-group living. And although you might experience it as a rather painful process, I propose to analyze these new methods in some detail to show some of the most overlooked complications of these methods. It might be important to say at this point that I do not try in any way to question or minimize the value of these methods. I only hope to point out the many hidden traps of which we have to be aware in order to avoid them.

1. Dialogue and depression.

The word dialogue is used here in a very general way. It is meant to embrace many forms of behavior described in terms such as: encounter, open discussion, talking things through, being open to each other, and it indicates a high level of verbal communication. In this analysis we want to focus on the verbal aspects of the dialogue.

The growing emphasis on the value of verbal communication of students with each other and their faculty is based on two usually unarticulated presuppositions which are usually taken for granted. They are, first, that free and open sharing of ideas and feelings brings people closer together, and, secondly, that a high degree of verbal interchange facilitates existential decisions by clarifying the issues involved.

Our first question therefore is: Does verbal communication bring people closer together? Although words are meant to communicate, they very often are used as a curtain to prevent communication. You probably remember that one of the best ways to succeed in an oral exam is to keep talking to prevent the professor from asking more questions, or to keep him talking, allowing him to suggest the answer before you have to confess your ignorance. In many discussions words are used to fill a fearful silence, to prevent the real questions from being asked or the painful issues from being touched. Many parliamentary discussions are aimed more at delaying the problem than at coping with it. Hours of talk in the United Nations, which to an outsider seem trivial and artificial, fulfill the highly useful function of preventing a dangerous encounter. Although this seems obvious on a large scale we seldom are aware of these same dynamics if we encourage our students to discuss their problems. But let us not forget that students who are constantly subject to grading and evaluation are in many ways afraid of each other and usually hyper-self-conscious. They are often so caught up in questioning their own adequacy that they are hardly open to allowing anybody to enter into the sensitive area of their personality, where they experience doubts and confusions. When you observe a discussion of students carefully, you will often find yourselves in the midst of many verbal harnesses, which are often more restraining the more words are used. If you don't believe it, just see what happens when someone is interrupted. The only one who usually brings the subject back to the moment of interruption is the speaker himself. Very seldom someone else says: "Sorry, you were talking about your trip through the mountains when John came in. How did things go on?" If the storyteller himself does not pick up the subject again, the conversation shifts to other subjects without pain.

What do people do when others are speaking? Well, very often they are busy preparing their own story, or deciding upon their own position. If someone remarks: "The assassination of Senator Kennedy was the result of a communist conspiracy," the usual reaction to that statement is the internal question: "Do I agree or not?" Instead of trying to better understand the speaker's position, the listener is thrown back on himself, and is busy figuring out his own position. And as soon as this position is verbally expressed, the rest of the dialogue is often a constant attempt to defend it, and to avoid defeat. Very often you will see people convincing themselves and their peers of an idea which they only hesitantly formulated in the beginning. The sadness of this story is that people often enter the discussion freely and relatively open-minded, and leave it very opinionated, with the meager satisfaction that they could not be convinced of the opposite and that they won a battle even when there was basically nothing to win.

All I am trying to say is that verbal interchange between students does not always bring them closer together. It might just as well separate them. Seminarians who have been encouraged to dialogue with the suggestion that this will create a better community can become very disappointed and even hostile when they find that a year of discussion did not take away their feelings of loneliness and alienation. Often enough they find an unexpected contrast between the result of many discussions and the main reason why they engaged themselves in the first place. And sometimes they feel more like strangers after than before the dialogue started. It is not difficult to see how a feeling of failure and depression can come forth from this experience.

Our second question is: How far does the clarification of pertinent issues help to solve existential problems? Here we touch a very painful source of frustration. For insight into a problem and the ability to cope with it are two different things. If seminarians discuss the meaning of the priesthood, celibacy, the institutional church, the death of God, etc., this might help them to think more clearly about these issues and to see the different ramifications of the problems, but if they expect to solve their very personal questions: Should I become a priest, live a celibate life, remain within the institutional church, and believe in a living God, then long discussions can become an excruciating experience. I have followed a year-long discussion by seminarians who hoped to make a decision on celibacy before the approaching date of the ordination. It was sad to see how these students became more and more entangled in a complex net of arguments, ideas and concepts and found themselves lost in a labyrinth of theological turnpikes, highways and sideroads, with a growing anger that they never came to that mysterious center where the answer was supposed to lie waiting for them.

What is really happening here? What would you think about a boy and a girl spending an hour a day to find convincing arguments that they love each other? You know these discussions are the best argument that they should not marry each other, if they don't want to enter into a rigid, stiff relationship, with a total lack of spontaneity.

Discussion requires a certain distance from the subject which allows you to see the many aspects of the issues, and gives you the opportunity to be analytical about it. But analysis means a temporary delay of participation. And only on the level of participation, existential decisions are made. Nobody becomes a priest because of three or four convincing arguments. Nobody commits himself to the celibate life because of Rahner, Schillebeeckx or Sydney Callahan. Theology, psychology and sociology don't offer solutions for existential crises, and everyone who suggests this enhances frustration, especially in the case of young men who have not yet fully experienced the limitation of the ratio.

There is a tragic and humorous note to the fact that, whereas in many seminaries there is a growing adoration for explicit intellectual awareness and an increasing emphasis on "knowing what you do," the nonreligious youth is burning incense, practicing meditation, and eating seed, to reach a higher degree of participation with the basic sources of life. Meanwhile our liturgies have become more talkative and verbose, and incense and other stimuli, auditory and visual, are scorned as being a part of an old magic.

But what we see is that the seminarians feel caught in the ropes of their dialogues and, seeing no end in terms of decision-making, they become disappointed, moody and depressed.

2. Small group living and depression.

Besides a growing emphasis on dialogue and discussion we find in many formation programs a shift from large, sometimes anonymous, groups of students living together in one building, to the more intimate, small groups, which often are called teams.

The team approach is an obvious reaction to a very impersonal kind of living in which the students went through many years of formation without ever being able to establish meaningful relationships with their fellow students or faculty. By dividing the large group into small teams, the possibility of real fraternities is created and a new form of community living envisioned. But here also, just as in the case of dialogue and discussion, things don't always work out in the expected direction. Let us try to understand some of the difficulties involved with the team approach.

a) The first problem is the simple fact that seminarians cannot avoid each other any longer. In a large group, where small, informal subgroups usually develop, there exists the possibility of staying away from irritating people, of keeping distant from others who seem to operate on a different wavelength, and of moving more or less freely in and out. In a team you are very close to a few fellows, and many of your activities are under the critical eyes of your team members, even when you don't feel attracted to them. If you do not show up at a team meeting, this not only will be noticed, but also criticized as a sign of lack of interest or commitment to the group. If you do not speak in a gathering people wonder why you are so silent. Whatever you do or don't do can become highly charged by very personal connotations. It is obvious therefore that team living is much more demanding than living in a large group, and asks for a much greater maturity.

b) The second problem is related to the confusion about the meaning of a team. The word team is usually used to indicate the cooperation of a small group of people who by coordination of their different skills are better able to fulfill a certain task. The common task is what determines the nature of the team. If the team does not function well, this will be reflected in the quality of the work.

In a formation setting, however, the team often is not task-oriented. The team wants to create the best possible living conditions for its members. It is more like a family unit to which you return after a busy day of work. And here the problems start, because the team in this setting easily becomes self-oriented instead of task oriented, and the problems of the team are not any longer related to questions raised by the nature of the work to be done but to questions raised by the nature of the interpersonal relationships. And in this case many team meetings tend to degenerate into amateur group therapy, in which members try to explore their feelings toward each other, and encourage each other to put on the table many things which much better could remain in the drawer. Team meetings in this case can become highly charged, and instead of moving away from individual concerns to a common concern, they can become self-centered to the point of narcissism.

We have to realize that the students involved are already very self-conscious, considering their age, their academic life and their ambivalent feelings toward their future profession. And although it might be very important that individual anxiety and confusion be expressed at certain times, the main purpose of the whole formation is to encourage students to grow away from this self-interest and to become free and open, to be really interested in the life and concerns of their fellowmen.

It is true that a culture which does not allow regression at times can ruin people. Without sleep man cannot live, but the real things usually don't happen during sleep. Crying, talking about yourself, and defenseless expression of feelings of love and hate are very important for the mental health of man, but they all are temporary regressions which can only be meaningful in terms of an ensuing progression. In formation regression should be allowed and even encouraged at times, but never considered as an ideal to strive for. The ideal remains not to be concerned with yourself, not to cry, not to express all your emotions, but to forget your own problems, and to do the work which calls for your attention and interest. Therefore, I feel that a team in which regressive forms of behavior are encouraged is vitiating its own purpose.

c) This brings us to the final problem with the team, which is related to intimacy. Lonesomeness is often experienced on a very deep and painful level by adolescents and young adults. The tendency exists to look for a solution to this problem by establishing very demanding and often exhausting friendships. These friendships can be clinging and immature and based on primitive needs. One of the tasks of formation is to stimulate the student not to let himself be guided by these impulsive needs, but to come to a mature self-awareness and self-confidence, in which friendship can develop as a giving and forgiving relationship and in which feelings of lonesomeness can be understood and accepted in a mature way.

Therefore it is very important to prevent the team from becoming a clique which is allowed to act on primitive needs and desires. This is difficult because the stresses on many students are so intense that they often have inexhaustable needs for intimacy, and clinging friendships. But this is often encouraging the unrealistic fantasy that the true, real, faithful friend is somewhere waiting, able to take away all the feelings of frustration. A man who lives in the seminary or enters the priesthood with this fantasy is doomed to be a very unhappy man. And if the team becomes a way to satisfy this unrealistic desire for intimacy, much harm can be done.

So we can see that team living is a very special and delicate enterprise which demands the special attention of those who are responsible for formation. The main danger is that a task-oriented team degenerates into a self-oriented clique in which sticky relationships drain the psychic energy of the students and allow regressive behavior. In this situation students easily become peevish, very demanding and irritable. They tend to ask for more attention than anybody can give and for more sympathy than anybody can show. They speak more about love than is healthy, enjoy in a very subtle way their own loneliness, and show basically all the symptoms of a spoiled child. And the most common universal and contagious symptom of this regressive behavior is depression, the feeling of not being understood, loved or liked, and the desire to be pitied by those for whom they feel a strange mixture of hostility and love. And so small-group living can easily, in complete contrast with its intention, degenerate into a very depressing way of living. Most remarkable is that the feelings involved are often so vague and all-pervasive that the seminarians themselves and even the staff have great difficulty in identifying the source of the problem.

Appendix: *The problem of fatigue*

Before finishing this diagnostic section, I would like to consider one of the most visible symptoms related to the problem of dialogue and small-group living. A remarkable number of seminarians complain about an inappropriate degree of fatigue. Although they can sleep as long as they want, they look very tired. Their eyelids feel heavy and they experience their bodies as something they carry around. The philosopher might say: "They have their bodies more than they are their bodies." When they wake up in the morning they don't feel relaxed, but are very much aware of them-

selves lying on the bed as a heavy load. Even dressing becomes like a job that asks concentration and special energy.
This so-called neurotic fatigue is the result of a way of living
which is characterized by hyperawareness, by which man
does not rely any longer on his automatic processes, but
wants to know what he does from moment to moment. Just
as a man who wants to be aware of his breathing is in danger,
and one who wants to control his heartbeat cannot live, a
seminarian who speaks all the time about friendship, love and
community might miss the opportunity to experience any of
these realities. This lack of participating life is usually related
to an often unconscious anxiety. Somehow man in that state
of fatigue has temporarily lost his basic confidence that life
is good and worth living and acts as if he has to be constantly
awake, always prepared for unexpected traps and dangers.

This form of fatigue can be harmful because it easily
brings the students into a vicious circle which he can hardly
break. His depression makes him tired, and his fatigue makes
him depressed, and so on. I do not want to suggest that all or
most seminarians show this symptom, but some of them do,
and recognizing its nature might prevent us from saying:
"Come on, take a good rest and don't study for a day," because instead of helping him, that sort of advice might make
it worse.

This finishes our diagnostic section, in which we discussed
the problem of depression as a problem of identity of students
and staff and as a problem related to the new educational
methods, dialogue and small-group living. As an often visible
symptom of depression, we focused on the neurotic fatigue.
All this leaves us with many questions. The temptation now
is to say: "Perhaps we should go back to the good old days,
with the early hours, long meditation, the rites of discipline

and the whole clearcut system of reward and punishment."
Before we make that mistake we should raise the question
of therapy.

II. THERAPEUTIC CONSIDERATION

After our rather long diagnosis we might wonder if the
new trends in seminary education are really as promising as
we hoped them to be. If openness to many basic questions,
the new democratic forms of government, the emphasis on
dialogue and small-group living result in a funereal atmosphere or a collection of intelligent grumpies, we could become somewhat suspicious about being modern.

But this is a temptation, the famous temptation, of using
the weak spots in renewal as an argument for conservatism.
If anything is clear it is that the seminary life as we knew it
ten years ago is gone, never to return. And what is even more
clear is that it took courage, imagination, and a great sensitivity to our changing world to start new ways in the preparation for the priesthood and the religious life. And it would be
easy, cheap and dishonest to point to the mistakes of those
who took the risks of new experiments. Every form of experimentation is bound to yield some unexpected problems. If
they were expected, it probably was not a real experiment
to begin with.

But we also have to try to account for the problems. And
when we explained how new student-staff relationships and
new educational approaches have their painful drawbacks,
we did not want to suggest that the new ways are the wrong
ways, but that they can perhaps be smoothed a little bit by
a better understanding of the dynamics involved.

Therefore, our task now is to formulate an "antidepressive regime," that is, guidelines which might help to allevi-

ate the depressive reactions to many creative initiatives. Before mentioning, however, any specific guidelines we should formulate the principle on which all guidelines rest. That principle is that all formation has as its primary task to offer a meaningful structure which allows for a creative use of the student's energies. Structure is the key word of formation and the criterion of any educational guideline. Structure allowing one to judge which feelings to trust and which feelings to distrust, which ideas to follow and which to reject. Structure providing unity to the many seemingly disconnected emotions and ideas of the student. Structure which helps to decide which plan is just a fancy and which contains the seed for a workable project. Structure, which offers the possibility to organize the day, plan the year, and steer the course of life.

Our problems today are not related to the fact that we are too modern, too liberal or too progressive, but that we do not have as yet the meaningful structures through which we can help the student give form to his many as yet undirected and unfocused potentialities.

In the context of this principle we now will try to formulate some guidelines. We will do this in terms of student-faculty identity and in terms of the new educational methods.

A. Structure and the identity problem

A student who is struggling with his identity in terms of competence, control and vocation will never find this if the staff to whom he daily relates does not claim in a clear and defined way its own role. This role is a role of authority. If a staff member has no authority at all a student cannot relate to him as a student. The main guideline here is that the staff has to be authoritative without becoming authoritarian. Authoritative simply means that the source of the staff member's authority lies in his competence, maturity and faith. He knows his field, is able to cope with the tensions of life and believes that he is called to do a meaningful work. This is the kind of authority that is inner-directed and does not need to rely on quotes from popes, bishops or superiors in order to give a sense to desires. An authoritarian man needs the rules to live, an authoritative man lives in such a way that the rules become obvious. Students want to be criticized, reprimanded and even punished. They ask for it if you can hear their language. But the authority by which this happens should be based not on subjective feelings and ideas, not on abstract rules and regulations, but on a critical, competent and objective understanding of the students' behavior.

Conflicts, frictions and differences of opinion don't have to be avoided. They are a part of formation. But only when the faculty claims its own authority and insists on it, will the student be able to identify himself, evaluate his own experiments in life and take a firm stand there where he feels solid ground. And such a student is not depressed.

B. Structure and the new educational methods

Our second guideline is related to dialogue and small-group living in the seminary. Both are highly moral activities which require someone who is able to take the responsibility. If it is true that a discussion can unite as well as separate, and that a small group can be task-oriented as well as self-centered, we are involved in very sensitive areas of life which cannot be left to the process of trial and error. If nobody accepts this responsibility, emotions, ideas and plans will be like water which is not guided by a riverbed but splashes in all directions destroying land instead of irrigating it. He who accepts responsibility will be able to provide creative channels through which life can become purposive. Therefore our guideline here is that such sensitive processes as dialogue and group living require a well-defined responsibility in order to be effective.

This responsibility usually means that some form of leadership has to exist by which structure can be brought to dialogue and group processes. Let me mention different ways in which this leadership can function.

a) Good leadership can prevent group processes from becoming amateur forms of group therapy. The expression of love and hate, anger and frustration, hostility and erotic desires, without special control, careful supervision and well-defined goals is dangerous and tends to harm people more than help them.

b) Good leadership can foster at times of crisis the right atmosphere to discuss certain existential issues. Such a discussion can have a temporary value. When the leader is not just an equal participant, but represents more than an individual opinion, he can make it clear to the students that they are on safe ground and they are protected against dangerous traps.

c) Good leadership keeps the communication in a group free and open. Nobody can be forced to enter a discussion if he does not want it. Many people just don't have anything to say or are not ready to say it. And subtle pressure to participate in a dialogue can take away the freedom of people to determine their own degree of intimacy.

Considering these aspects of good leadership it seems that the essential idea is that discussions and group living can only bring people closer together if they are already together in some way. Leadership means the representation of some level of community within which these processes can take place in a creative way. The leader's authority can be seen as an expression of the authority which belongs to the community in the first place. The task of a leader, therefore, can be seen as safeguarding the boundaries of the community and judging which ideas, feelings and actions can be handled within these boundaries and which not. And people will feel much freer to express themselves when they know that they will be warned when they trespass.

Therefore, good leadership offers an antidepressive regime by bringing the loaded question into the safe context of a community. And this brings us to our conclusion which finally allows us to ask what a religious community can be.

The Religious Community

After these "therapeutic" considerations in which structure was the key word, we finally had to bring in the term community. Perhaps this is the most widely used term in recent discussions about religious life evoking feelings of great excitement as well as feelings of utter boredom. Up to this point we have tried to avoid this word in order to take a more critical look at the underlying dynamics. But by way of conclusion we need to bring this big word back to our attention and ask ourselves what it means in the context of the problem of seminary depression.

Religious community is *ecclesia*, which means called out of the land of slavery to the free land. It is constantly moving away from the status quo, searching for what is beyond the here and now. As soon as the community becomes sedentary, it is tempted to lose its faith and worship the house-gods instead of the one true God who is leading it in a pillar of fire.

If we speak about vocation we have to ask first of all if the community has a vocation that means experiencing itself as being called out of Egypt, the land of depression, to a new as yet undiscovered country. It seems that some communities have lost their élan and have become so enchanted by the beautiful oasis which they found on their way that they settled for that and forgot their real call.

I think that the vocation of the individual seminarian can be seen as a participation in the vocation of the community. When many students leave the seminary these days, this might very well be due to the fact that they have not been able to find the vocation in which they can participate. Instead they found a group of people very preoccupied with internal conflicts, wrapped up in small, insignificant debates about rituals, rules and authorities, and remarkably blind to the fact that most of their energy is spoiled by trivia while the world is on the verge of committing suicide. These self-centered communities tend to throw the student back on himself and encourage him to be very reflective, suggesting that vocation is an internal inspiration which cannot be discovered unless through endless self-scrutiny. This causes the seminarian to take himself much too seriously and to ask his superiors to pay constant attention to his most individual needs and desires. I think that the problem usually is not with the students who want to give their best, nor with the faculty who are willing to do anything for their students, but with the community at large, which has lost its most basic conviction that its existence is mandatory because it is called to fulfill a task nobody else will fulfill.

There is no lack of generosity. There is so much of it that everyone who can mobilize it and channel it can make mountains move and oceans hold their waves. I am convinced that a community which feels called to do a most difficult task, which asks for great sacrifices and great self-denial in order to do the work of God which is obvious and self-evident, will have no problems at all in finding people who want to join in the challenging enterprise. He who promises hard work, long hours, and much sacrifice will attract the strong and generous but he who promises protection, success and all the facilities of an affluent society will have to settle for the weak, the lazy and the spoiled. It is sad to say, but it is not always the weak and the lazy who leave our seminaries, but often the strong and the generous who had too much to give to do their best in an easy life.

The task of the religious community is to constantly move away out of the comfortable situation and to look for areas where only one who is willing to give his life wants to go. This can be everything: education, hospital work, mission work, etc. But as soon as any of these enterprises starts to become very profitable and successful we should know that this is a state of temptation and a challenge to cut the ties again, and to move on to new areas. And much of the depression we discovered in our diagnosis might be considered in the final analysis as a sign that the community is tempted to stop being *ecclesia* and to lose contact with the pillar of fire. A religious community can only survive when it stays in contact with this fire. It is the same fire which was the symbol of the new community on the day of Pentecost. Instead of huddling together and clinging to each other in fear, the apostles opened their doors, stepped into the world and went out in different directions. They knew that they were carried and supported by more than just the psychological experience of sympathy and friendship.

That is what Jesus indicated to the hard-headed Peter when He asked him three times: "Do you love Me more than these others do?" Jesus meant *agape*, not *phileia*. It took Peter a while to understand the difference. But Jesus meant that only this Divine love, *agape*, would make it possible for him to fulfill his vocation. Because this vocation meant that he would not any longer put on his own belt and walk where he liked, but stretch out his hands and let somebody else put a belt around him, and take him where he would rather not go (John 21:18). Only by growing old would Peter be able to do this. The formation in the seminary is meant to allow this growth to the mature man who strengthened by the new love is able to understand that the cross is no longer a sign of depression but a sign of hope.

Intimacy and the ministry

6

The Priest and
His Mental Health

If you were ever present at the admission of a severely disturbed patient to a mental hospital, you might have been
surprised by some of the questions asked by the psychiatrist.
Instead of asking: "What is the problem?" or "What is
bothering you?" he sometimes says: "Can you tell me what
time it is, do you know what day it is, what month is this,
what year is this?" Then he inquires: "What is the name of
this town and what country are we in?" And finally he asks:
"What is your name, who are your friends, and what job do
you have?"

Why does a doctor ask all these obvious questions? He
wants to know if the patient knows: when he is, where he is,
and who he is. Because basic to man's mental health is that
he is oriented in time, place, and person, or—to say the same
—that man is realistically aware of himself.

But what is most basic to our mental health is also crucial
in all levels of our behavior. The painful and difficult problems in our life are always related to essentials. We cannot
exist without being loved, but nevertheless to love and to
be loved remains our main concern through life. In the
same way, being oriented in time, place, and person is
at the root of our mental health. As we grow up and are

confronted with new bits of reality every day of our life, this remains a constant challenge, especially for those whose world is in the midst of turmoil, subjected to severe reevaluation and extreme self-criticism. That is our world, and perhaps especially the world of the priest. The question: "When, where and who am I?" might after all not be easy to answer when asked by the priest in the modern world. Suddenly and painfully confronted with new and confusing realities, he might lose his orientation. And this means that his mental health is threatened.

Therefore, I will discuss the mental health of the priest in the world in terms of healthy timing, healthy spacing, and healthy self-understanding, and show how problems in these three areas can become a source of mental suffering for the priest in the modern world.

1. Healthy timing

Healthy timing is perhaps one of the most obvious and nevertheless least understood problems for priests. Let us have a look at two forms of timing: long-range timing and short-term timing.

Long-range timing refers to the way a priest uses his days, weeks, and months in the perspective of an effective life plan. I don't think that it is an exaggeration to say that many newly ordained priests leave the seminary with great ambitions, high aspirations and often zealous expectations. The excited new priest tends to jump into his pastoral activities as a true follower of Pelagius. He very soon can become the victim of what by distant observers has been called "A redemption complex." He is almost omnipresent, as far as his territory goes. No Bible group, no P.T.A. meeting, no Boy Scouts practice, Holy Name gathering, social, financial or pious meeting exists without his being there. He talks with almost everyone who wants to talk with him, gives advice to troubled parishioners, counsels couples, teaches classes to grade, trade and high school, and is constantly available for everybody's needs, except perhaps his own. He seldom refuses an invitation, seldom says no, and seldom withdraws to his private room. And he receives his rewards. He is popular, well-liked by his parishioners. They call him nice, kind, and understanding, and say: "This man is really giving himself for his people. He at least understands what is going on. He is different from the old pastor. This young man is available for us, all the time." Indeed, all the time. With a certain pride he tells his colleagues that he hardly gets more than five hours sleep a night, that he never has an opportunity to read a book except his breviary, that he does not even have an hour free to play a game of golf.

Well, you know what this is: The redemption complex in full bloom. But how long does it last? Two, four or five years, perhaps, then things start to look different. He has not been able to change the world around him as he had hoped, people are not so much different from the way they were during his first year. The same old problems keep coming up, but they don't look so exciting anymore. No new books or ideas have entered his room. Then, slowly, but sometimes very pervasively, a feeling of dullness and boredom can creep in and the question comes up: "What am I doing after all? Nothing is really changing and I am getting tired of activities, people, and myself."

Fatigue—physical, because of lack of sleep; mental, because of lack of motivation; and spiritual, because of lack of inspiration—takes over and leads to neutral resignation, growing irritation, or even to eroding depression.

We can call this unhealthy long-range timing. The so-popular, inspiring, creative priest has become, in a few years, an irritated, empty, routine, tired man, who keeps repeating to himself, if not on the pulpit, that since Jesus Christ nothing really has changed, and that there is nothing new under the sun. And many priests who were the hope of the diocese or the star of the order become bitter and disappointed men; some clinging to the priesthood to keep some sort of a home, others leaving it in the hope of starting a new life somewhere else.

But this is still somewhat exceptional. Much more common is the unhealthy short-term timing. Short-term timing refers to the way a priest uses his hours during one day. It seems to me that it is extremely important that the priest has a time to work and a time to relax. There are ways of living in which it is difficult to say whether a person is creating or recreating. A priest who lives in the rectory all day and is surrounded by his colleagues, in a way, is always in his office. People can call him every hour of the day and he is never completely outside the work atmosphere. On the other hand, he can rest at very unusual hours and is always also in his home where he eats, sleeps, plays and prays. So there is very little definition of time. This can result in a feeling of being always busy day and night, without really either working hard or resting well. He has some scheduled activities, but otherwise his work is pretty well at random. The priest is never very certain about what he will be doing during the next hours. To a man with a high sense of duty, this can become extremely frustrating. The lack of gratification can result in a feeling of: "I did not do enough" and impels him to do more in his free hours, with the effect that his disappointment with himself only increases.

When the distinctions between day and night, work and play, duty and hobby, become fuzzy, life loses its rhythm and becomes poorly defined. Such "unhealthy living" may kill inspiration and creativity by making a man the victim rather than the organizer of his time. He is always on the go and seldom stops to reflect on the meaning and effectiveness of his busy life. And sometimes it seems that he is afraid to stand still and think, afraid to discover that being busy and tired is quite something else from being useful.

It is clear that this problem is closely related to celibacy. A priest never leaves home to go to work and never comes back after having fulfilled his daily task, to find someone who helps him take some distance. He is always at home and never at home; he is always at work and never at work, and he wears his uniform always without any distinction of time or kind of activity. This unhealthy short-term timing also can soon lead to fatigue as a constant complaint and to boredom as a constant mood.

In short, healthy timing is essential for the physical, mental and spiritual health of the priest, not only in terms of the long-range effectiveness in his life as a priest, but also in terms of his creativity and inspiration in daily life.

2. Healthy spacing

Besides a healthy use of time, a healthy use of place is of great importance for the mental health of the priest. We can speak about healthy spacing. Seminarians, diocesan and religious priests mostly live in houses where they share all the various aspects of their lives under one roof. One of the critical problems of the Catholic seminary today is called its "total institutionalization." This means that every level of living of the student—his religious formation, his academic training, his social life and his physical education—are all institution-alized and under the same roof, the same rule, and the same authority. The one, very defined milieu pervades and covers all the levels of the life of the student.

And this is not only true of the seminary, but in many ways also of the religious community life and of the rectory life. It seems that there is only one organization which can compete with the Catholic church in terms of total institutionalization, and that is the military.

The priest or seminarian often finds himself in a situation which is experienced as suffocating. If he eats or drinks, plays or prays, sleeps or stays up at night, studies or day dreams, goes to a movie or to a play, all his activities are directly or indirectly under the same authority. He is enclosed.

One of the reasons why a man in the business or academic world is often able to tolerate considerable frustration is exactly related to the fact that he does not find his demanding boss back in his private home, that in his interracial committee he can be leader; that if he goes on a vacation with his wife and children he has authority and responsibility which is different from his authority and responsibility in his profession; that when he goes to the country club he can temporarily forget his conflict with his wife and his problems with his kids. In other words, there are different roofs under which he lives: his home, his office, his cottage, his country club, his church, all representing different realities of life with different authorities and responsibilities. They indicate different levels of living, not completely separated, but distinct enough to be able to function as a mechanism to prevent, compensate, or take away many strains and pressures of daily life. If your superior is bugging you, you at least don't have to face him all day. If you always have to smile and be nice as a tourist guide, you at least can be mad and angry at home for a while. If you cannot say what you think about your secretary in your office, you at least have a chance to let your steam off with your friends in the bar. Different places and different spaces. That can create a healthy balance.

The seminarian or priest often lacks this variation. Whatever he thinks, feels, does, says or writes is finally under the critical eye of the same authority or string of authorities. A parish pastor not only expects his assistant to do responsible professional work between 8 and 5, he also wants him to play bridge with him once a week, to socialize with some of his friends, to join him for a dinner party and perhaps even play golf with him. But he also may expect him not to drink too much beer, not to see *Blow-up*, not to talk with prostitutes on the street, not to wear a tie, not to buy a Thunderbird, and not to receive girls in his room. This is what might be called spiritual suffocation and causes many seminarians and priests to feel caught in a web of unclear relations from which they cannot free themselves without tearing loose. Leaving the priesthood can then become a way to get some fresh air.

Closely related to healthy spacing is the problem of authority vs. responsibility. The question is: "To what extent are we boss under our own roof?" First of all, in the Catholic church we are very quick to delegate responsibility but very slow to delegate authority. Many sermons, lectures, and talks are aimed at convincing us of the tremendous responsibility of the priest in the modern world. But the authority which belongs to this responsibility is not always a part of the package. A priest is responsible for the good atmosphere in the house, but he cannot always change the rules; responsible for a meaningful liturgy, but he cannot experiment very much; responsible for good teaching, but he has to follow the prescribed sequence of subjects, and especially responsible for good advice, but he does not feel free to give his own opinion because he has to represent someone else's authority instead of his own. In reality, this means that in a setting of total institutionalization every sphere of life is controlled from one central point. This has its advantages. After all, the general of an army cannot win a war if he has only partial command over his troops or if that command only lasts from 8 in the morning until 5 in the evening. The question for a priest, however, is whether he is really at war.

But there is another perhaps more complicated problem. That is the problem of the shadow government. Those who have authority do not always know how much they really have. Often they suffer from lack of clarity. The superior of a house does not know how far he can go because a bishop is watching him somewhere; the bishop does not know how far he can go because the apostolic delegate is looking over his shoulder, and the apostolic delegate is not sure exactly what Rome thinks. The problem is not that some have more authority than others, but that there is no clarity and that the further one gets from the problem the thicker the clouds become. Perhaps a lot of fear and anxiety about authority is not so much related to power but to the cloudiness of power, which leaves the responsible people always hanging shadowy in the air. Nobody knows who is really saying what and the further away from home the vaguer and the more anonymous people become. This is what I mean by the shadow government, which causes this constant referral to eternity, where all lines melt together in a quasi-sacred mystery that cannot be touched.

In short, healthy spacing not only refers to healthy defining of places and rooms, but also, connected with that, to healthy clarification of responsibilities and authority which belong to the different roofs under which we live.

3. Healthy self-understanding

But after all this, we still have not arrived at the core of the matter. More fundamental than healthy timing and healthy spacing is healthy self-understanding. In this tumbling and changing world the priest is faced with the most central question: "Who am I?" The rapidly diminishing number of vocations to the priesthood all over the world is dramatically showing that along with the whole church, the priest has entered into an identity crisis. He is asking himself: "Who am I and what can I do?"

In discussing the priest's reality orientation in terms of person, we will make a distinction between his individual and his professional identity.

A. If someone's individual identity crisis concerns the basic levels of his personality he suffers from a severe pathology. Deep depression, obsessive compulsive action, and different forms of psychotic behavior indicate that psychiatric help and sometimes hospitalization are needed. Although perhaps few priests suffer from these severe forms of identity confusion, this basic problem is, in some degree, the problem of every man—but perhaps more of every priest.

How does the priest see himself in his relationship with his fellowman? How does he relate privacy to fellowship, intimacy to social intercourse? Essentially, human existence is "being together." I am not alone in the world but I share this world with others. To be able to live a healthy life in this world which judges me and asks me to play a role according to my physical identity, two things are necessary. First, that I must have my own inner privacy where I can hide from the face of the challenging world; and secondly, I must establish a hierarchy of relationships with this same world. In the inner circle of my life I find him or her who is closest to me. Around this circle of intimacy I find the circle of family and dear friends. Then, at a somewhat larger distance, I locate relatives, and acquaintances and, even further away, the associates in business and work. Finally, I am aware of the vast circle of people that I don't know by name but who in some vague way also belong to this world, which I can call *my* world. Thus, I am surrounded by expanding circles on the threshold of which I station guards, who carefully check whom they allow to enter into a closer intimacy with me. I don't say to the bus driver what I can say to my colleagues. I don't say to my friends what I can say to my parents. But there is a place where nobody can enter, where I am completely by myself, where I develop my own most inner privacy. This is the place where I can meet God, who by His incarnation has thrown off his otherness. The possibility for a man to hide from the face of the world is a condition for the formation of any community. A man who does not have privacy cannot be a part of a community.

It is exactly here that the priest has problems. Very often he has lost his private life, where he can be with himself; nor has he a hierarchy of relationships with guards on the thresholds. Being friendly to everybody, he very often has no friends for himself. Always consulting and giving advice, he often has nobody to go to with his own pains and problems. Not finding a real intimate home in his house or rectory, he often rambles through the parish to find people who give him some sense of belonging and some sense of a home. The priest, who is pleading for friends needs his parishioners more than they need him. Looking for acceptance, he tends to cling to his counselees, and depend on his faithful. If he has not found a personal form of intimacy where he can be happy, his parishioners become his needs. He spends long hours with them, more to fulfill his own desires than theirs. In this way he tends to lose the heirarchy of relationships, never feels safe, is always on the alert, and finally finds himself terribly misunderstood and lonesome.

The paradox is that he who has been taught to love everyone, in reality finds himself without any friends; that he who trained himself in mental prayer often is not able to be alone with himself. Having opened himself to every outsider, there is no room left for the insider. The walls of the intimate enclosure of his privacy crumble and there is no place left to be with himself. The priest who has given away so much of himself creates an inexhaustable need to be constantly with others in order to feel that he is a whole person.

And here the priest is in a crisis situation. Without a spiritual life and a good friend he is like a sounding brass or a tinkling cymbal. This might impress you as an old-fashioned sermon, unless you realize that the question underneath is: "Who guides him who has to guide his people?" No psychotherapist will feel competent to help people if he himself is not willing to constantly reevaluate his own mental health with professional help. But which priest has a spiritual director who helps him to find his way through the complexities of his and others' spiritual lives? There are hundreds of priests who are able theologians, good preachers, excellent organizers, brilliant writers, highly competent sociologists, psychologists, mathematicians and philosophers; but how many are there who can help their fellowmen and especially, their fellow priests, in their most individual spiritual needs? Those seem to be as seldom as white crows. Perhaps one of the most urgent questions remains: "Who is the pastor for the priest?"

B. This brings us to our final and perhaps most specific concern, the professional identity of the priest. Healthy self-understanding not only means a healthy understanding of yourself as an individual in the world, but also a healthy understanding of yourself as a professional man.

The first and most obvious question seems to be: Do we actually have a profession? We live in a society which is characterized by a rapidly growing professionalization. We see a growing number of professionally trained people: doctors, psychiatrists, psychologists, social workers, lawyers, judges, architects, engineers, and nearly every year new professions seem to create themselves. In the psychiatric field we now speak about music therapists, group-therapists, occupational therapists, etc. Everyone has his own specialty, with his own training and his own place in the team of the professions. Where does this leave the priest? What is his speciality? What is his own unique contribution? Is it not true that many priests feel extremely frustrated because they feel that they know a little bit of everything but are not really good in anything? Many feel that they are amateur counselors, amateur social workers, amateur psychologists, amateur group leaders and amateur teachers, but when and where are they really pros? And it is not surprising that many priests are very uncomfortable in a professional milieu, and, in spite of their four or five years of post-graduate training, feel more at ease with the so-called "simple people."

Priests have pretty good reasons to feel this way. A doctor, after four years of theoretical training, needs at least two years of internship under close supervision before he is allowed to practice by himself. A psychologist cannot start his independent work before at least two years of practical training in a very controlled supervisory setting. A social worker does not earn his title without many years of very strict guidance in his professional field. But what about a priest? Most priests study four years of theology and then jump right into the pastoral work without any internship whatsoever. And of those who have a pastoral year only very few receive the needed supervision to make their experience in practice a real learning experience. Who supervised their sermons carefully? Who critically studied and discussed their pastoral conversations? Who helped them to express in the liturgy something meaningful through their hands, voice and eyes? And especially, who helped them to consider the relevance of their knowledge and information—stored up during four years of theory—for their very specific relationship with the confused teenager, the searching college student, the doubtful husband, the despairing father or the depressed widow? Who helped them to ask if their pastoral expectations are realistic or if their desires and needs are tolerable? Who taught them to make intelligent choices and accept possible failures? Who explored with them their limitations, and who taught them to handle the complicated authority problems in relationships with superiors as well as with parishioners? Who inspired them to do more study and research in their own field, and who finally guided them in the integration of new experience? In short, who made them real professionals?

The sociologist, Osmund Schreuder, writes: "The crisis in regard to the priesthood in our time seems to be related to the professional underdevelopment of this occupation."[1] If this is true, we face a mental health problem because a man who permanently doubts his own competence can hardly be considered mentally healthy.

A second question is: Even if our work is professional, is it a rewarding profession? A professional man who works hard and is creative, receives his rewards. People tell him how they appreciate his work. They praise him, give him a higher salary, and offer him a promotion. And the visible and tangible rewards make him appreciate his profession more. What about the priest? Many priests seem to experience their work as simply filling a position which happened to be open. They are not there because of the specific professional skill which they can apply to that specific situation but they are there because no other priest was there for the job. And once in the job, nobody really cares what he does. As long as he doesn't do stupid things, does not write letters to the editor and does not generally disrupt the existing order, he doesn't hear anything. The reward of the quiet priest is silence from above.

Few religious authorities praise their men. They expect them to do their job and not to ask for a "thank you." Perhaps many priests have even denied themselves the desire to be praised, thanked, paid and appreciated. Some distorted view on obedience seems to forbid a desire for gratification and satisfaction. It is amazing to see how few priests can

---

[1] Osmund Schreuder, "Het professioneel karakter van het geestelijk ambt" (*Dekker en van de Vegt*, Nijmegen 1964), p. 7.

accept a real compliment. They are not used to it and feel somewhat embarrassed, as if they are not allowed to be complimented. But when all the gratification you get out of your study is your grades at the end of the semester, you are less mentally healthy than when you enjoy your study daily and have a good grade on top of that. Daily life in the latter case, is fun. In the former case, you have a lot of pain for the sake of a little gratification. If a priest does not enjoy his daily pastoral work and is only hoping for God's grade at the end of his life, his mental health is in danger. And so is his most important task of bringing life and happiness to his fellowman.

There is one form of gratification which is most absent in the daily life of the parish priest, and that is the gratification of his professional theological discipline. Every professional man knows that his task is not only to keep informed in his field, but also to offer a creative contribution to it. The doctor and psychologist know that while working with people they are helping them best when at the same time they are looking for new insights for the sake of their discipline. A doctor who sees hundreds of allergic patients might, by a systematic way of treating them, not only serve his patients but also his science.

Are there pastors who realize that the people they are working with every day form one of the main sources for their theological understanding? Since God became man, man became the main source for the understanding of God. The parish is just as much a field of research for the priest as the hospital is for the doctor. Perhaps nobody made us so much aware of the need of this empirical theology as the Protestant mental-hospital chaplain, Anton Boisen, who wrote: "Just as no historian worthy of the name is content to accept on authority the simplified statement of some other historian regarding the problem under investigation, so I have sought to begin, not with ready made formulations contained in books, but with the living human documents and with actual social conditions in all their complexity."[2]

The priest is confronted every day with living human documents, and if he is able to read and understand them and make them a constant source for his theological reflection, his life can always be new, surprising, inspiring and creative. There is no human problem, human conflict, human happiness, or human joy, which cannot lead to a deeper understanding of God's work with man.

In this way his profession asks him to remain responsible for God, to keep God alive always changing and always the same, as man himself. And it is here that the priest can find himself at the heart of his profession.

Healthy self-understanding. This was our last and main concern. Healthy understanding of our own individual self realistically related to the other on the basis of a sound spiritual life and a sense for intimacy, and healthy understanding of our professional self, which gives us a humble, gratifying, and scholarly place in the team of the helping professions.

This brings us to the end of this orientation session. Is the priest oriented in time, place and person? Does he know

---

[2] Anton Boisen, *The Exploration of the Inner World* (Harper & Brothers: 1962), p. 185.

when he is, where he is and who he is? Our roaring days are threatening his balance, balance between private and public life, between places to be reserved and places to be shared, between contemplation and action, between study and work. This threat creates anxiety. And this hurts. But if the wounds are understood, it might very well be a constructive anxiety. Then an honest diagnosis serves a good prognosis.

7

Training for Campus Ministry

During the Second World War, many army chaplains, Protestant and Catholic, were faced with a very difficult question: How to be a pastor without a church? In the field there is no pulpit to speak from, no altar to stand behind, no bible class to direct, no discussion group to lead. Many felt like carpenters who had lost their tools. They had to ask themselves, "Can I do something without anything but myself? Can I be a priest without a collar, a book, or a chalice?" In this emergency situation, thousands of men ran to the quickly organized seminars to get some basic training in this new field work.

Perhaps our University campuses today are like the battlefields of the Second World War. The familiar channels through which we could function and reach thousands of students, are leaking or completely broken down. Religious bulletins, processions, rosaries and holy hours are strange memories that evoke a smile. Chapels have become less popular places to visit. Masses and other celebrations only attract a small section of the campus population. Bible clubs, discussion groups, and retreats are liked, perhaps by many, but we wonder for how long. And as time goes on we feel ourselves victims of a religious strip tease in which students are insisting we remove one vestment of office after another, as if to say: "We want to see you naked, and then we will see what you are worth."

In short: We cannot rely on old channels and prepared roads, but we are thrown back on our most personal resources and faced with a great deal of anxiety. To use the image of Erwin Goodenough: The curtains through which we communicated with the divine, are torn down and we wonder if we can live without them.[1]

In the middle of this confusion we ask for training. But can we speak about training if we are not clear about its object? What does it mean to be a campus minister? If we are able to delineate the role of the campus minister, we also will be able to lay bare the main areas for training. Therefore, I propose first to raise two questions closely related to one another.

1) How can the priest be an efficient and skillful pastor in a campus community?

2) How can he remain a whole and integrated man in a milieu which is constantly changing and by its own nature repeatedly challenging his own commitment?

You will probably realize that the second question is much more important than the first, however seldom asked. But let us start where the question is asked and then break through to the level where it hurts. Then, finally, we are free to ask the last question.

3) What is the best way to prepare a man for this special ministerial task?

---

[1] Erwin R. Goodenough, *The Psychology of Religious Experiences* (Basic Books: 1965).

I. The Efficient and Skillful Campus Minister

Although the faculty and other personnel related to the university also ask for his attention, the main pastoral concern of the campus minister is the student. We will focus on the pastoral care for the student.

For most students, the patterns of life were pretty clear and well-defined during their high-school years. Home and school were closely related and many customs, practices, rules, and regulations, although often criticized in their particular form, were seldom questioned on a basic level. There were many problems, but problems could be solved. There were many questions, but every question had an answer. There were many stupid teachers, but the smart ones knew what they were talking about.

But at college things became different. Being away from home, without strong anchors in the family tradition, and without a clear goal on the horizon, the student starts drifting. Familiar answers do not work anymore, long cherished beliefs lose their obviousness, and carefully built structures crumble, sometimes suddenly, sometimes gradually. And in this new milieu where science sets the tone, where research is the main approach and hypothesis the main model, certainty becomes the most suspected attitude and the question-mark, the most respected symbol. But asking questions is a fearful thing. The answer might be No. Do I have anything to hope for in my future? Yes or No? Is love a real human possibility? Yes or No? Is there anybody who cares for anybody except himself? Yes or No? And finally: Is life worth living? Yes or No? Asking these questions is a dangerous thing to do. Many may prefer to stay away from them and do their daily business because it seems much safer to hold

to "the way they think and act at home" than to rock the boat
in such a stormy sea. But if the student used to the micro-
scope, familiar with Skinner boxes and proud of his com-
puter techniques, avoids asking these questions about the
core values which give meaning to any tool at all, he takes
the risk of becoming an unhappy genius, a man who knows
everything except why he lives.

It is in this milieu that the campus priest has to be a pastor.
What should he be able to offer to the student? I propose to
discuss this under three titles: *a climate, a word, a home.*

1. *A climate*

Perhaps the real desire of many students is not primarily
to find an answer to the deep and often painful questions
related to the meaning of being but to find a climate in which
he is allowed to ask these questions without fear. Most amazing about many Christian milieux is the great taboo on asking
questions. You know how questions about the divinity of
Christ, the virginity of Mary, the priesthood of women, the
advisability of abortion, and even about a good selection
process for bishops might not be just food for an interesting
discussion but would spoil many meals in a rectory. These
questions seem to be more than interesting; they are dangerous and explosive. Questioning the morality of war, the value
of academic progress, the meaning of monogamy may cause
people to throw stones through your windows because all
these questions suggest that the safe little playpen we have
set up for ourselves might be nothing more than a subtle
form of self-deception. But if we are so afraid to face a question which comes from without, how much more threatening
will the question be which comes from within? Is it really
worth eating and drinking, studying and fighting, living and

being? We know that the most common form of mental suffering on campuses today is depression. Depression is caused by questions which cannot be asked and which are swallowed and inverted into the experience of deep guilt. The question, "Why do I live?" is turned into a castigating self-doubt, "Is it worthwhile to live?"

Can the priest tolerate this question? Can he offer a climate in which the most basic doubts can be expressed without fear, where the most sacred realities can be unveiled without creating the need to defend, where despair can be allowed to be despair without the need to fill the threatening holes? Can he accept agnosticism? That is, can he accept the fact that we do not know the reality in which we live? A man who lives in a scientific milieu has to learn to be happy with a little bit of knowledge. Goodenough states: "The true agnostic is not interested in whether man can ever 'know' the truth as a whole; what he wants is to find out a little more than he knows now."[2]

If Christianity is not a panacea for every doubt, ignorance, and impotence, it might create the possibility of being an agnostic without being afraid, of being happy without a cure-all and safe without a playpen. Gordon Allport considers as one of the attributes of a mature religion *"its heuristic character."* He writes, "A heuristic belief is one that is held tentatively until it can be confirmed, or until it helps us discover a more valid belief."[3] If this characteristic can develop anywhere, it should on a college campus. But what is needed is a climate to allow searching without fear, and questioning without shame. The first demand of a question is not to be

---

[2] *ibid.*, p. 182.

[3] Gordon Allport, *The Individual and His Religion* (Macmillan), p. 72.

answered but to be accepted. Then the problem of faith can become the mystery of faith and the problem of God, the mystery of God. As long as the priest considers atheism as the only alternative for orthodoxy and unbelief as the only alternative for dogma, every question put to him will be felt as a threat and every doubt as an attack calling for defense. But his faith tells him that growth can only take place when belief and unbelief, doubt and faith, hope and despair can exist together. It is only slowly that a student is willing to realize this, and he will never be able to do it unless there is someone to offer him a fearless climate.

2. *A word*

Many have already said, since St. Paul, that faith comes from hearing, and that the word of God is all we have to give. But few were wise enough, as was St. Paul, to realize that not every word is for everyone, that some need milk and others solid food. Diagnosis has been one of the weakest qualities in the pastoral field. What doctor would give all his pills to all his patients? What psychologist would administer all his tests to all his clients? What counselor would give all his advice to all his counselees? Their training is geared to diagnosis, based on the insight that not everything is good for everyone, and that help only can be given on the basis of the clinical understanding of the unique needs of our fellow-man. But it is sad to see that so much pastoral activity is based on the supposition that all the good words are good for everyone. And often the pastor behaves like a poor sales-man who wants to sell the whole church as a package at once to everyone he happens to meet.

Much pastoral phoniness is related to the inability to be clinical in pastoral contact and pastoral conversation. Not everyone needs encouragement, not everyone asks for correction, not everyone is ready to be invited to prayer or to hear the name of God. Some ask for silence, some for a single word, some need instruction, some just understanding, some want a smile, some a severe hand, some need support, and some need to be left alone. Perhaps much of today's anticlericalism on campuses is related to the insensitivity of men whose vocation is to care for the most individual need. If anybody is aware of his own individuality and unique needs, it is the student who is studying to find *his* place in *his* world. The fact that many prefer a psychologist to a priest is less related to the different ideas they have to offer than it is to the fact that the one thinks diagnostically and clinically and the other often globally and generally. And therefore, the campus minister should be able to offer a word which is an honest response to the unique and highly individual needs of the students.

3. *A home*

The third and perhaps most difficult thing to offer is a home where some degree of intimacy can be experienced. In our modern highly demanding, and competitive university, which is everything but a Schola—a place to be free—many students suffer from an intense feeling of loneliness. They are very self-conscious, constantly on their watchtower to register carefully all the movements of their surroundings, hyper-alert to the reactions of their teachers and fellow students. They have their antennas out to pick up all those signs which can suggest the way to good grades, good letters of recommendation, good grad schools, and good jobs. For many, it has become a matter of life and death because they know that if you can't carry books, there will be little else than rifles to carry. Many experience some sense of self-contempt and have lost the ability to be with themselves. In this highly stress-filled situation, intimacy has become nearly impossible for many students. And although in this searching time of life there is a heightened desire for warmth, tenderness, and disarmed relaxation, for many students their roommate is more a stranger than a buddy, their classmates more rivals than friends, their teachers more authorities than guides. This craving for intimacy is perhaps one of the most central concerns for the campus minister. How can he, in some way, somewhat satisfy this nearly inexhaustible need?

The answer is obvious but at the same time immense. It is the creation of a community where the student can experience some sense of belonging. If the years of free search are not surrounded by some form of intimacy and lived in some form of community, the search may be bitter instead of mild, narrow-minded instead of mature, cold and calculated instead of open and receptive.

There are many ways in which we have tried and do try to form these communities: discussion groups, weekends, retreats or advances, many forms of celebration and most of all the Eucharist. Crucial to all these forms seems to be the creation of a healthy balance between closeness and distance. The campus minister can be the guardian of this very subtle balance. This is very difficult because the need for intimacy can be so strong that it finds expression in a suffocating embrace. Different forms of intense mutual confession, sharing of feelings, and repeated physical contact may seem a good sign on a campus which counts so many alienated students but, in fact, can create cliques instead of community, stickiness instead of freedom, and even fear instead of love. In this desire to experience some oneness, students might cling to each other instead of freely communicating. And if the campus minister sees a growing interest in Pentecostalism, Cursillos, group-dynamics, and very informal liturgies, he should not only ask himself to what extent do these new groups satisfy obvious present needs, but also to what extent will they offer in the long run the freedom and maturity the student is looking for.

In the many new experiments in liturgy on campus, the balance between closeness and distance seems to be essential for the maturation of the Christian. A good liturgy is a liturgy with full participation without a pressure to participate, a liturgy with free expression and dialogue without an urge to be too personal, a liturgy where man is free to move in closer or to take more distance without feeling that he is offending people, and a liturgy where physical contact is real but does not break through the symbolic boundaries. I don't think there will ever be a single good liturgy. The personality of the minister, the nature of the students, and the climate of the place ask for many different forms. But much more important then the particular format, canon, language, or gesture is the careful balance between closeness and distance which allows the Christian community to be intimate *and* open, to be personal *and* hospitable, to receive the daily core-group as well as the occasional visitors, to be nurturing as well as apostolic.

The problem of intimacy is very often experienced as the core problem of the emotional life of the young adult. His relationships with female as well as male friends often can be clouded by painful anxieties. Closeness is desirable as well as fearful, and it asks for a careful guide to find a vital balance which can lead to a life in which one can be committed and open-minded at the same time.

Summarizing the special skills which can make the campus minister 'an efficient and skillful pastor we might say: He should offer a climate, in which the student can raise basic questions without fear, a word which is an honest response to his individual needs, and a home where he can experience intimacy with a vital balance between closeness and distance.

II. THE SPIRITUALITY OF THE CAMPUS MINISTER

But all we have said until this moment seems rather trivial and superficial if we consider it just in terms of skills for efficient ministry. I hope you have already become aware of the fact that, all the way through, the minister himself is involved most personally, most individually, and often most painfully. If our real concern is the making of the "whole man," "the mature Christian," we cannot avoid the question: How can the minister himself become and remain a whole and integrated man in a community which is constantly changing and by its own nature constantly challenging his commitment?

In many ways the campus community is the most demanding and tiring place for a minister to work. Every four years his parish is completely de-and-repopulated. Each time he is once again faced with a new wave of searching, questioning, critical men and women who usually have mixed feelings when they are invited to contact the priest. Over and over again, he is asked to respond to the powerful feelings of doubt, aggression and loneliness and to act as guide in the intensive struggle for self-discovery and meaning in life. This means a constant request for honesty, authenticity, openness, and a nearly bottomless availability. And when he finally, often after a long time, has received confidence and established some community, he will find that graduation is often the end of it all. Students go away and keep going away. The minister stays. Except for some cards at Christmas, he does not hear very much any more and thanks are seldom expressed. He knows that students have to leave; he even knows that they should not become too attached to the school or to him and that an education to independence sometimes also includes a renunciation of thanks; but he also knows how much it hurts when people, in whom he has invested so much of his own self, leave him. How often can a man build with care and patience a personal relationship with people who will be running away so soon only to look back at their college years as a part of their necessary preparation for life? For the student, college is just a temporary phase; for the minister, it is a way of living. And finally, how much questioning can a man take? Can he allow people to ask him all the time: Why are you a priest? Why do you believe in God? Why do you pray? Can he allow himself to be flexible all the time and willing to shift gears, to incorporate new ideas, to scrutinize new criticism and to question again his basic convictions? But this is exactly what happens, when students ask questions because every question about the meaning of life is, at the same time, a question about the meaning of the ministry. The question, "Why do I live?" is at the same time the question, "Why are you a priest?" It is obvious that not only the student but also, and perhaps even more, the minister realizes that his own existence is at stake.

If it is true that a psychiatrist who works closely with people in conflicts has to watch his own emotional life very carefully, then this is even more the case for a priest who is in daily contact with ultimate questions of life and death. And just as X-rays can heal and hurt us, exposure to these questions can have good but also dangerous effects. It is not so surprising that campus ministers are often suffering from a considerable amount of stress and need serious pastoral care more than anybody else. Although every campus minister has his own personality and therefore asks for individual guidance, there seem to be some main problem areas which allow generalization. We will discuss these under three titles: silence, friendship, and insight.

1. Silence

A university is not only a place for intellectual pursuits but also for a good amount of intellectualization; not only a place for rational behavior but also for elaborate rationalization. It is probably not only the most verbal place but also the most wordy and talkative place. And religion is not exempt from this phenomenon. The campus minister is exposed to a nearly unbelievable amount of words, arguments, ideas, concepts, and abstractions. How can he separate the sense from the nonsense, the holy words from the crazy ones? This problem is tremendous not only for the student but just as much for the minister who might fall into the temptation of adoring the products of man's consciousness, trying to catch even the divine in the net of his explicit awareness. He can become entangled in the ropes of his own sentences and unable to be moved by the great Power which is beyond his capacity to articulate.

And often the drama of the campus minister is that, trapped by the need to understand and to be understandable, he loses communication with the realities which—as he himself knows—are transcendent to his mind.

In this context the campus minister needs silence. Silence means rest, rest of body and mind, in which we become available for Him whose heart is greater than ours. That is very threatening; it is like giving up control over our actions and thoughts, allowing something creative to happen not by us but to us. Is it so amazing that we are so often tired and exhausted, trying to be masters of ourselves, wanting to grasp the ultimate meaning of our existence, struggling with our identity? Silence is that moment in which we not only stop the discussion with others but also the inner discussions with ourselves, in which we can breathe in freely and accept our identity as a gift. "Not I live, but He lives in me." It is in this silence that the spirit of God can pray in us and continue his creative work in us. We never will find God in students unless it is God within us who recognizes Himself in them. Without silence the Spirit will die in us and the creative energy of our life will float away and leave us alone, cold, and tired. Without silence we will lose our center and become the victim of the many who constantly demand our attention.

2. Friendship

The second urgent need of the campus minister is friendship. Here we enter a very difficult area because it is the most sensitive one. But it has to be said that the campus minister who depends for friendship on students is in a very dangerous situation not just because of the fact that students will leave him after some years but more because friendship with students often paralyzes the possibility of being their pastor. If the student community becomes the main source of the personal gratification and satisfaction of the priest, he easily becomes the victim of fluctuating sympathies and preferences and quickly loses his freedom. If he needs students to fill his emotional needs, he clings to them and is not able to maintain the distance which allows him to be different. And as soon as students experience his great desire to be intimate with them, to know details of their lives, to be invited to their parties and closely involved with their daily ups and downs, they lose the possibility of relating to him in a creative way.

The campus minister needs privacy, a home where he is not with students, and where he is free for himself. Just as no doctor could stay healthy if he would only see patients, and no psychiatrist could stay "whole" if his private life and that of his clients would merge, so no campus minister will ever be able to function well over a long period of time if he would always be with students. It might seem that student problems are urgent and that they require immediate attention, but let us first of all ask ourselves, "Do they really need us more than we need them?" The campus priest needs a home, a place where he can live with friends and have his own intimacy. Only then will he keep from drowning in the high and low waves of the fluctuating life of the university.

3. *Insight*

Besides silence and friendship, insight is one of the main constituents of the spirituality of the campus minister. By insight, we mean a sound perspective of the minister on the significance of his own priesthood. Although much suffering of today's priests derives from distorted emotions, we should not overlook the importance of a clear understanding of his task in the society of today. For many priests, it is not so much their needs for friendship and sympathy which limit their pastoral freedom as their theological outlook on their own existence. I just wonder how many guilt feelings of today's priests are related to their concept of God, their view of revelation, and their ideas about Jesus Christ and his church. If the campus minister thinks that *he* is responsible for the faith on campus, if he thinks that it is his task to bring as many students as possible to the sacraments, and if he thinks that the students' way to heaven is somehow related to their membership in the church, he can be sure that the campus is going to be his purgatory. Because not only can feelings influence thoughts, but thoughts can also create very deep and powerful emotions. In the mind of a priest for whom sacramentality is, in practice, identical with the reception of the sacraments, the growing unpopularity of confession and communion must create a considerable amount of anxiety and perhaps even self-reproach. For a man to whom the recognition of Jesus Christ as Savior is the criterion of the fruitfulness of his priestly service, a modern college campus cannot do anything but cause deep-seated guilt feelings and much unhappiness. And if the satisfaction of the campus minister is dependent on a growing conversion of students to his creed and belief, his work can hardly be more than suffocating.

Many priests are deeply concerned today. Faced with the rapid changes in church attitudes, they worry and even panic, sometimes to the point of declaring the days as wicked, the students as degenerate, and Christianity as burning its last candle. The question is: Are these concerns really pastoral concerns, or are they rather more signs of little faith? Perhaps we are too easily caught in the narrowness of our own theological insights. They can make us anxious instead of free, unbelievers instead of faithful, suspicious instead of trustful.

Can the priest dedicate himself fully to a so-called non-religious student without the hidden condition or hope for a future conformity to his belief? In an academic community, people are very sensitive to the slightest form of pressure—hyper-sensitive even. The most guarded freedom is the freedom of thought. Although we are committed to God-*Logos* who came to free us from the God-*Anangke*,[4] that is, to the Word of God who liberated us from the chains of our pressing needs, it is very difficult to allow God's Word to be completely free. Often we do not feel comfortable with a free moving Spirit and prefer a so-called realistic limitation and control. But the Truth is to set us free. A growing insight through study of the Word and a deepening understanding of our own task as witnesses of this Word can prevent us from being a victim of our own narrow-mindedness.

Silence, friendship, and insight are three aspects of the spirituality of the campus priest which seem important if he wants to become and remain a "whole" and integrated man. If he wants to be a skillful and efficient minister who can offer a climate, a word, and a home for his students, he will soon find that without silence, friendship, and insight his fruitfulness will be very short-lived and temporary.

III. TRAINING FOR THE CAMPUS MINISTRY

The two questions, how to be skillful and how to be whole, proved to be closely related. Together they not only delineate a picture of an ideal, perhaps utopian, campus minister, but they also circumscribe the main fields of training. This brings us to the final question: How should the training of the campus minister take place?

There are many settings in terms of time and place within which we can envision a training situation. We can think of

---

[4] Sigmund Freud: *The Future of an Illusion* (Doubleday Anchor Books. New York), p. 97.

a one-day-a-week program extending over a whole year, of a series of intensive workshops, of a full-time summer program, and ideally of a whole year of pastoral internship.

Programs of this nature preferably should be planned on the campuses. If this is not possible other training fields, such as general and mental hospitals, educational centers, prisons, and industrial schools, could also be considered. But essential for every setting is that it offers supervised pastoral experience, that is, pastoral experience which through careful control becomes available for supervision by a competent and specially educated pastor.

Many future ministers are like people who have learned Spanish in school. They are able to read and perhaps even to write Spanish, but when they come to Mexico the best they can do is stutter. What they need is not just experience but also someone who constantly corrects their mistakes, makes them aware of their own idiosyncracies, and suggests new ways of expression according to the culture in which they find themselves. Experience without supervision can lead to the adaptation of poor patterns of behavior which are very difficult to shake off. It can create narrow-mindedness because it tends to make us settle on the first thing which seems to work. Then the pastor becomes like the conceited foreigner who says: "As long they know what I am saying, who cares what mistakes I make?" But this just might be the reason that he always will remain a foreigner. Pastoral work is more than a language. It asks for our ability to touch the most sensitive areas of life, and requires us not only to understand the highly individual needs of the other but also the many complex responses of the self. Just as no surgeon would start operating after only having read books, no pastor should touch the soft and tender internal life of his fellowman with the great books and the powerful ideas he brought with him from the classroom. Let me give you an example:

A young deacon in Holland paid a house visit to a middle aged couple and explained to them in convincing terms that birth control was no longer any problem, that they had no reason to be concerned about their son who had stopped going to church, that celibacy would go out the window within a decade and that most devotions were perfect examples of magic. After his exposition the mother of the house thought for a while and then said meditatively: "Nothing really has changed." "How do you mean?" asked the deacon. "Well," she mused, "twenty years ago the priests told us what we should do and believe. Now, with the same intolerance, they tell us what we should not do and not believe. After all the problem is still the same."

If this deacon wants to be sensitive to the real needs of his parishioner and if he wants to come to a better understanding of his own preoccupations he will be helped by supervised pastoral experience. Let us have a closer look now, first at the nature of the supervisory process and secondly at the kind of pastoral experience which can become available for supervision.

A. *The nature of the supervisory process*

It is obvious that supervision is a very delicate art, which not only requires sensitivity, and a special understanding of the dynamics of the human relationships, but also demands careful preparation for the difficult task of individual professional guidance. It is sad to say that within the field of Catholic pastoral education there are only very few men who can claim for themselves the title of pastoral supervisor.

To show the importance of supervision we will look at three of its characteristics.

1. An antiprojective regime.

First of all supervision is an antiprojective regime. The most striking characteristic of supervision is the constant invitation to take back our projections. The center of attention is the trainee. And although the trainee might explain his problems easily as the problem of the older pastor, the rigid institution, the unfatherly bishop, the anticlericalism of the students, the supervisor will ask him: "But what about you?" There are many ways to project. But seldom are we made aware of our inclination to draw people or situations into the picture behind which we can hide ourselves. What the supervisor does is to bring us right back to the center of the problem: me.

2. A school for alternatives.

Secondly, supervision is a school for alternatives. Every pastor has his own strengths and qualities. It is obvious that he will use and develop them as best he can. One will feel at ease in the pulpit, another in the classroom, a third in youth groups and a fourth in individual counseling. The question is whether our qualities might not become temptations to narrow us down to only those fields to which we feel most inclined. Professional training means a training which broadens our ways of pastoring and offers us possible alternatives. It gives us the freedom to act differently in different situations based not just on our inclination but on the understanding of the particular situation. Through supervision we are invited to face the weaker aspects of our behavior. The supervisor is saying: "There are many ways of being a good pastor. I know that this is the way in which you feel most comfortable, which is most easy to you, so let us forget this way for a moment and have a look at other possible ways." If a man uses his strong capacities too much he is in danger of having his other potentials become paralyzed or at least underdeveloped. If he feels too much at ease with a specific pattern of behavior the danger exists that the learning process will stop.

Supervision never gives lasting satisfaction. It is an ongoing process of opening new possibilities. This opening is a most painful process. It gives you the feeling that everything can be done differently and that it is at least immature not to consider the other possibilities.

Therefore, supervision seems to be only consistent in its inconsistencies. It forces one constantly to move away from what is safe. It is a very frustrating process. The supervisor often seems to consider his student as cream. He doesn't mind in what direction he churns him, he's only interested in the butter which is the result of all his stirring.

As a school for alternatives, supervision creates distance. It says: "Stop, have a look at yourself, and think." The tendency to act on the spur and the impulse of the moment is so great that blindness to alternatives can result. But after good supervision we know at least, that although we are taking one road there are other roads which we did not choose. We know that distance is possible without causing separation, and that involvement is possible without causing blindness.

3. The way to basic questions.

Finally, supervision is the way to ask the basic questions. Supervision is not a problem-solving device in which the supervisor advises his student what to do in difficult cases. It rather offers the freedom and opportunity to ask the basic questions. Very often the minister invests much time and energy in problems which are peripheral and accidental, without questioning the suppositions on which his actions are based. Many problems can be used to hide the real question. The question: What should I say to this student? can cover up the question: Why do I want to say something to him at all? The question: How can I reach as many students as possible? can cover up the question: Why should I reach so many students? The question: How can I make the liturgy attractive? can hide the question: What does attractiveness mean when speaking about liturgy? The question: How can I be a good witness for Christ? can disregard the question: Does Christ really mean anything to me? And finally the question: How can I be a good priest? can avoid the question: Do I really want to be a priest? Through supervision we might finally have the courage to touch the heart of the matter and to ask the basic questions. And this brings us back to where we started: Asking basic questions is the privilege of the mature Christian. So we see supervision as an antiprojective regime, as a school for alternatives and as a way to ask the basic questions.

B. The pastoral experience

But what has to be supervised? That is our final problem. The answer seems simple: pastoral experience. But how does pastoral experience become available for supervision? By control, by creative limitation. Franz Alexander calls psychotherapy a controlled life experience. Training for the ministry can very well be called a controlled pastoral experience. Doing many different things can be helpful as well as damaging, but doing just a few things under close supervision is priceless. Talking with hundreds of people about God may be fine, but analyzing one conversation word for word is a learning experience. Not only learning how to talk, but also learning how to understand myself in the interaction with my fellowman. The great importance of pastoral training is the opportunity for the minister to experience himself as a professional person in a controlled setting. To struggle with one's own professional self in a situation in which every aspect of one's daily ministerial practice becomes subject to supervision is a way of learning, unique and practically unknown in the tradition of Catholic theological education. It is especially the controlled experience which makes this pastoral experience different from so many other experiences in the field.

About a decade ago some Hollanders started to build a miniature Dutch city in which the tallest church tower did not come higher than a man's waist, the famous public buildings of the country were knee-high, the great rivers could be crossed in one step and the whole world in which we live could be overlooked in one glance. This miniature city soon became one of the greatest tourist attractions and not just for children as was planned, but for adults as well. The sensation seems to be the controlled life experience. People suddenly were able to see themselves as a part in a larger setting of which the structure and the boundaries were visible. This is what makes supervised pastoral experience so exciting. It is a pastoral experience in miniature, through which we are able to see where we stand and where we go. If we want to prepare ourselves to live and work in the complex university community it is important to start by looking at it from some distance and to make us familiar with the complex map of student life, so that we will not get lost, once we enter it fully.

We will finish as we started. The minister preparing himself for work on the campus is like an army chaplain entering the battlefield for the first time. Anticipatory anxiety is to be expected. This anxiety can paralyze efficient work and endanger the integration of the personality but by careful training this same anxiety can become constructive instead of destructive and a source of great pastoral creativity instead of distress. A minister who is prepared for his task can enter a university community even when it is in great turmoil, without fear. He is free. With a realistic confidence in his abilities, with a sense of inner harmony and most of all with the trust in the value of his service, he can be a free witness for God, who can strengthen hope, fulfill love, and make joy complete.

Conclusion

Intimacy was the main theme which brought together the otherwise so different subjects of this book. In the context of man's development from the magic oneness of the small child to the faithful oneness of the adult Christian we discussed the intimate relationships possible between man and woman, man and man, man and God. We also tried to show the problem of the student trying to find his own place within the religious community and finally we analyzed the situation of the contemporary minister who is called to guide others in their search for meaning without losing his own home.

It does not seem an exaggeration to say that this book was primarily concerned about the inner life of man. This might seem a somewhat unpopular emphasis in a time in which the social problems are so pressing that much attention for the "stirrings of the soul" easily suggests a pietistic preoccupation with the self.

But if man really has to love his neighbor as himself there seems to be a good reason to wonder if man today is able enough to relate to himself in a creative way and to live from the center of his existence.

During the past years many concerned idealistic men returned from their social actions in the fields, the ghettos and the slums with the painful realization that the courage to continue and the will to persevere can not depend on the gratification which they received from their involvement. There were hardly any visible results, very few words of thanks and not seldom suspicion and hostility. Many were thrown back on themselves and had to ask: "Why should I do all this, when nobody asks me to do it, when many call me naive, and when most people remain completely indifferent towards my great desire to make a better world?" The answer to this question will never come unless man is able to live from his center and feel at home with his own self. Consciously or unconsciously many young people practicing Yoga, reading Zen and intrigued by new forms of meditation are asking for a new spirituality and are looking for a guide.

The churches, in many ways entangled in their own structural problems, often seem hardly ready to respond to this growing need to live a spiritual life. The t.agedy is that many find the church more in the way to God than the way to God, and are looking for religious experiences far away from the ecclesiastical institutions. But if we read the signs well, we are on the threshold of a new area of spiritual life, the nature and ramifications of which we can hardly foresee. Hopefully, we will not be distracted by the trivia of churchy family-quarrels and overlook the great questions which really matter. Hopefully, we will be sensitive enough to feel the gentle breeze by which God makes His presence known. (1 Kings 19:13).